MW00880618

The Hawk Is My Ship

DONALD L. HOWE

Copyright © 2019 Donald L. Howe

All rights reserved.

ISBN: 9781796982787

DEDICATION

This book is dedicated to the men and women who maintain our freedom, and the unprecedented environment of liberty and ingenuity that keeps them better equipped than those who would destroy that freedom.

ACKNOWLEDGMENTS

I would like to acknowledge my son Scott Howe who edited the manuscript to get it ready for publication, and also all my family members who helped proofread and encourage me to complete the project.

THE HAWK IS MY SHIP

Nothing is quite as awesome as the first time one approaches an aircraft carrier. These ships are HUGE, to say the least, and I was very impressed. I was reporting aboard the USS Kitty Hawk, CVA-63, for duty as Assistant Air Operations Officer. I didn't know why I was chosen to serve on an aircraft carrier, as my experience had been with land based, multi-engine aircraft in anti-submarine warfare. I had landed aboard a carrier as a student pilot, as did all Naval Aviators, but other than that, I had never been on a ship. I resigned my thinking that sometimes the Navy did strange things, and this was probably one of them.

"The Hawk", as this ship became affectionately known, was BIG! As aircraft carriers go, it's not the biggest, but it's still BIG! It was hard to appreciate its 1000 plus foot length, standing on the pier, but I could appreciate its seven-story tall flight deck towering above. There seemed to be antennas, gadgets and machinery stuck all over, and sailors were scurrying about the ship busily going about their daily in-port chores.

I remembered from military etiquette classes that when you go aboard a Navy ship you climb the ladder onto the

"Quarterdeck", salute the ensign and the Officer of the Deck (OOD). Next you request permission to come aboard. I did this. The OOD returned my salute, welcomed me aboard, then introduced himself. He then excused himself and made a phone call. Soon an airman came to escort me to the personnel office. I followed him dutifully, not from an etiquette standpoint, but because as soon as we left the Quarterdeck, I became absolutely and totally lost! We walked across the quarterdeck, through a hatch into a huge cavern inside the ship called the hangar deck. Then across the hangar deck through a small hatch into a small passageway, down a ladder onto the main deck, down another long passageway, reversed direction and went up a very long escalator to the 03 level, reversed direction again, then down another long passageway through many hatches, turned left and finally reached the personnel office. My head was reeling from the climbs, descents, turns, escalators and a myriad of passageways. I was greeted by a Yeoman who took some of my papers (you always have a mountain of papers when you transfer in the military), gave me a check-in card, and wished me good luck. I thanked him and turned, pausing at the door, wondering if I would ever see daylight again in my natural lifetime! Amused, and knowing my bewilderment, the Yeoman assigned the same airman to escort me to the Air Operations Department, where I was to work. We then went through another maze of ladders and passageways that I won't even try to explain, until we reached AIROPS.

I met my new boss, the Air Operations Officer, and a few others including my new roommate and mentor, Tom. After chatting for a few minutes with my new acquaintances, Tom escorted me through our sister division spaces, the combat Information center, to our stateroom. The stateroom, home for the next 2-1/2 years, was a space about 8 feet by 12 feet, equipped with built-in lockers, desks, bunk beds and a wash basin. Once inside the room, I confided with Tom that I knew nothing about any ship, especially an aircraft carrier, and that I was totally lost and confused. I asked for his assistance in finding my way around. He graciously showed me some survival routes. First, the closest bathroom. Then how to get out of the ship into fresh air the most expeditious way, in case of fire. Third, how to find the closest place to eat. Finally, a quick way to get back to the quarterdeck and freedom! With this knowledge, I could survive.

My duty for next two days was to check-in.

My assignment aboard the Hawk was to become an Air Operations Watch Officer, more commonly known by the station call sign as AIROPS. In this position I would be responsible for coordination of all the air operations within a 50-mile radius of the ship, including launches and recoveries, planning for the future launches, controlling the ship's tanker aircraft, overseeing the Carrier Air Traffic Control Center (CATCC), and coordinating all aircraft emergencies. In short, it was a position of making the Air Operation work! Before reporting to the Hawk, I didn't even know such a position existed. Now I was to do this, even though I couldn't find my own way around the ship! I was to relieve another officer after a two-month training period. My roommate and mentor, Tom, held the same position. There was no formal training for the position other than being an aviator and CATCC training, which I had just completed that taught basic air control procedures. All other training was to be on the job.

Sometime during the next couple days, I met the Operations Officer (My boss's boss), The Executive Officer (Crew's Boss), The Air Officer (AIR BOSS), and the captain (EVERYBODY'S BOSS), and a host of other officers and men, most of whom I wouldn't recognize again until after our second or third meeting. I finished checking-in to the necessary places that served two purposes. Each office needed to know you were aboard, and wandering around in a state of confusion for a period of time, enabled you to figure out basically where you were. This procedure is like being plucked off the ranch and set down in the middle of New

York City. After you wander around long enough, things become somewhat familiar. I have to admit that I was on board the ship for about a year, with the ship having gone into overhaul before I really knew where I was. I did discover that if I could find the main deck or the flight deck, I could find where I needed to go, even if it was sometimes by accident.

The Mighty Aircraft Carrier is the heart of a task force designed to extend a government's political power far beyond its borders. It is equipped to go to sea for long periods of time and travel great distances all the while acting as an air station for the Carrier Air Group or Air wing. It is also a big and prized target. Thus, the carrier always plays both an offensive and defensive role, and its operations are conducted accordingly.

The Hawk's crew was divided into three groups. The first group was the ship's company, who run the functions of the ship, both as a ship and as an air station, commanded by the CAPTAIN. The ship itself only had one airplane assigned, the Carrier Onboard Delivery or COD aircraft. The second group was the Carrier Air Group or Air Wing, who operate and maintain all the aircraft except the COD plane. This group was commanded by the Carrier Air Group Commander or CAG. The Carrier Air Group was normally stationed at a nearby land base until just before the ship deploys. The third group was the ADMIRAL and his staff. All carriers are commanded by an admiral somewhere, but not all carriers have an admiral aboard, nor did the Admiral and his staff always stay aboard the Hawk. The Admiral locates where he can perform his function most readily. Theoretically, the crew is totally organized in a proper chain-of-command. The air wing people report to CAG, CAG reports to the CAPTAIN. Ship's people report to the CAPTAIN, and the CAPTAIN reports to the ADMIRAL. Everyone has a boss, who ultimately reports to the CAPTAIN (or Admiral). In practice, there are a few short cuts taken.

Just as important as the official organization of the ship, is the unofficial one that really gets things done. For example: Every division, squadron, etc., has their own "unofficial" supply man to get those much needed and sometimes hard to get items required to do the job. NO one will admit this person exists, but when an item is needed, the word is put out within the division, and the next day it seems to just "show up"! NOBODY asks where it came from, or who got it. It is just used to do the necessary job. Although most everyone within the division or squadron knows who has done the deed, there is an unwritten law that prohibits revealing same. Some would call this outright theft, and it was. But, it was never done for personal gain, just to get the job done more efficiently.

A similar working relationship exists between departments and individuals in conducting flight operations. Flight operations are always conducted in "REAL TIME", meaning the operation doesn't stop for someone to decide what to do. This real time concept dictates decisions be made and forthcoming as the flight picture unfolds. By regulation, only the CAPTAIN has the authority to make certain operational decisions, but working in real time often requires immediate decisions by pilots, AIROPS, and other support personnel. When this happens, the CAPTAIN is later informed as to what "he decided". It takes a while to learn these relationships (they are never written), thus it is difficult to step into a job, and do everything right the first time. When a decision had been made for the CAPTAIN, and he didn't like what was done, the decision maker most certainly heard about it. I learned this the hard way. However, once I earned the CAPTAIN'S confidence, he rarely disagreed with the decisions I had made.

In my travels around the ship I discovered that it had almost everything a person needed to survive, including a store, barber shops, a laundry, a television station with closed circuit TV throughout the ship, a library, a workout room, a hobby shop, movies nightly in the crew's and officer's mess, a radio station, a snack bar and about 500 other spaces used for offices, housing and a myriad of other military things. It was in effect, a small city. I also discovered that it had its limits. You could go fore and aft, port and starboard, up and down, but once you reached the edge, you couldn't go any farther. From this standpoint, I suppose it was somewhat like being in a minimum-security prison, only with a shorter sentence. I found out later it was worse! We didn't have visits by WOMEN!

CARQUALS

Flight Operations aboard an aircraft carrier is a very complicated event. The Hawk had about 5500 men aboard, most of whom were directly involved. The ship has to be turned into the wind, traveling with enough speed to launch and recover aircraft. It also has to have enough open water ahead to complete the launch and recovery operation. All flight operations were conducted from the flight deck.

Due to the limited space available, all aircraft have to be parked in the proper sequence before each launch, called "stacking". The Flight Officer has a large magnetic table shaped like the flight deck, complete with little model airplanes, all to scale, upon which he solves the problem like a big jigsaw puzzle. The Flight Deck Officer and his crew then take over and position the aircraft. At the same time, airwing personnel are preparing the aircraft, refueling, and perform line maintenance. In combat, weapons and ordnance have to be prepared, positioned and loaded aboard the aircraft. Pilots and crewmembers have to be briefed on their missions. The ship's own weaponry has to be manned and ready. All of this has to happen, and come together at the right time to make the operation successful, thus the ship becomes a very busy place.

Flying high performance jet aircraft is a complicated affair. Flying these aircraft off a moving ship has a set of problems all of its own. First, the deck of a carrier is not long enough for a high-performance jet to take off. This type of launch would be called a "DECK LAUNCH". The Hawk's C-1 COD plane (A propeller driven plane), was the only plane capable of deck launching. All other aircraft had to be launched from one of four steam catapults. Two catapults were located on the bow of the ship, and were called the port or starboard "BOW CATS". Two were located at the end of the angle deck or runway, and were called "WAIST CATS ". When an aircraft is catapulted off the ship it is called a "CAT SHOT".

I always found the cat shot to be the most exciting event of a flight! One has to fully brace himself and have the aircraft ready to fly before the catapult fires. When the catapult is fired, the aircraft is accelerated from zero to its flying speed in 126 feet, taking about 2-3 seconds. The experience is like riding Montezuma's Revenge at Knott's Berry Farm, only about four to six times harder. At the end of the shot, the aircraft is flying, totally separated from the ship and on its own.

The second problem high performance jet aircraft have is the approach and landing. In the approach, the pilot must position his aircraft such that it is lined up with the extended centerline of the runway, configured to land with the arresting hook, landing gear, and flaps down. He then flies the aircraft along the extended centerline until intercepting the glide slope. The glide slope is defined by a mirror system located on the ship, that shows the pilot a ball of light when he is on the slope. When the pilot makes visual contact with the ball of light he reports on the radio, "BALL" or "MEAT BALL". This tells everyone on the ship, especially the Landing Signal officer or "LSO", the aircraft is in the right position to land. The LSO then gives directions to the pilot, as necessary, until he reaches a point just short of touchdown. If the aircraft is in the proper position, the deck is clear and the LSO judges a safe landing can be made, he clears it to land. This is done by flashing a green light on the "Ball" mirror, and calling "CUT, CUT" over the radio. When the Pilot receives a "CUT", he adjusts power, depending on the type of plane, allowing the aircraft to touch down.

As the aircraft touches down, the pilot immediately adds takeoff power, including afterburners. If the plane catches an arresting cable called a "wire" (actually a heavy cable), it is slowed to a stop in 150 to 200 feet. This is called a "TRAP", After being stopped by the arresting cable, the pilot reduces the aircraft's power to idle, raises his arresting hook and taxies the plane to a safe parking area under the direction of the flight deck crew.

If the plane misses a wire, the pilot now has to immediately make a takeoff and fly again (this is why he adds full power at touchdown). This is called a "BOLTER". The pilot maintains full power and begins a climb. When the proper interval has been established with other aircraft in the landing pattern, the pilot turns the aircraft and sets up for another approach.

Prior to landing when at the "CUT" position if something doesn't look right to the LSO, he directs the pilot to take the aircraft around, called a "WAVE OFF". The pilot immediately adds sufficient power to make a climbing turn, clears the runway and sets up for another approach,

Since a flight off the carrier always requires a CAT shot and a TRAP, pilots must be proficient at performing these maneuvers. A great deal of time and effort is spent developing this proficiency, called Carrier Qualification or "CARQUALS". During initial CARQUAL phases, pilots practice at a land base using a mirror system and a short runway painted onto the larger runway simulating an aircraft carrier deck. This is called FIELD CARRIER LANDING PRACTICE. When a pilot is proficient at the field, he then comes to the ship for daylight, visual landings, then finally night/instrument landings.

Three days after I reported to the Hawk, the ship got underway for CARQUALS. Unknown to the pilots coming for landing practice was the lack of proficiency of many of us who were controlling them. Many of the ship's company were new, and like myself, had to learn their jobs as they worked. At almost every position, two or three people practiced.

In my position as AIROPS, there was very little to do during daylight visual CARQUALS. Our function was primarily to monitor fuel states of the participating aircraft. This was a function that we did on every recovery and was significant because of the rate of fuel used by jet aircraft. An F4 Phantom, for example, uses 100 pounds of fuel per minute during normal cruise operations. When the pilot uses afterburners, the rate increases to 1000 pounds per minute. Afterburners are used on every CAT shot and TRAP, not for a very long time, but enough to use up fuel quite rapidly. When a bird was getting low on fuel our job was to see it was taken out of the landing rotation and refueled. Another condition occurred when a pilot was having difficulty making a TRAP. At a certain fuel state, determined by the planes fuel usage and proximity of suitable land bases, these planes would be pulled from the landing pattern and diverted to a land base for refueling. This procedure was called "BINGO", or "BINGO FUEL". The Captain was the only one authorized to BINGO an aircraft, but in practice AIROPS made the decision, executed the command, then called the Captain.

When our pilots completed the daylight visual qualification they moved to the night/instrument phase of qualification. This was a completely different procedure up to the point of landing for the pilots and the ship, especially AIROPs.

During night/instrument recoveries, incoming aircraft were put into a holding pattern at a certain point away from the ship until the recovery commenced, called "Marshal". The aircraft were under positive control by the ship's Carrier Air Traffic Control Center or CATCC, under the supervision of AIROPS. Commencing at its expected approach time, each aircraft was brought down from Marshal at one-minute intervals, descending so as to arrive at final control position about four miles out from the ship, on centerline and on glide slope. The pilot was then talked down by a final controller until on very short final where the LSO took over and the pilot landed visually. This procedure took a lot more time to execute, therefore the number of aircraft was usually limited to 12 or 14 per recovery.

During CARQUALs the procedure was altered somewhat if the weather was good, to allow more actual landing practice. The planes were brought down from Marshal for their first approach. After TRAP the aircraft were taxied to the BOW CATS and launched. The aircraft were then maintained in a long, racetrack pattern, with their turns to the "downwind leg" and "final approach" directed by a controller, all the while under positive control by CATCC. As the planes TRAPPED on their subsequent landings, they were again taxied up to the bow cats, and shot off, establishing a constant launch and recovery cycle.

CATCC, like everyone else, had many new people to train. Only an air controller would understand the nightmare they went through on that first night of CARQUALS. It would be like the first scrimmage of the season for a pro football team. Some individuals were brilliant, but as a group they looked like pop Warner. Fortunately, the pilots never knew, and I won't tell. But, providence was with them, and they got all the birds into the pattern. The weather was "clear to the moon", so the pilots were able to help and keep the operation from becoming one massive mid-air collision. After the third or fourth wave of planes, CATCC started to get it all together. Soon they were operating like a well-oiled machine.

My job was in part to make sure CATCC did their job correctly. To do this I had to maintain a mental picture of where each aircraft was in the pattern, what their fuel states were, coordinate any emergencies that may develop, and answer any questions from whomever on the ship. I was learning BINGO fuel states for each type aircraft we had aboard, what their emergency procedures were and who to call to get advice or information. I was sure it was not humanly possible to learn everything that had to be learned, in the time allowed. Looking back, I'm not sure how I made the grade. I felt like an idiot, and was sure everyone else thought that also. The nights were very long. Little did I know that CARQUALS were like child's play compared to what lay ahead.

One thing I did learn was to trust in my own intuition after weighing recommendations from those around me, regardless of their rank. The Operations Officer had a favorite practice of joining the Captain on the bridge during flight operations. While there he would listen for distress calls. When he would intercept a distress call he would immediately call AIROPS (who coordinated all emergencies) and, in the presence of the CAPTAIN, gave orders to solve the problem. Unfortunately, the solution offered was made without all the information at hand and was usually wrong.

One night, very early in my career aboard the Hawk this situation developed. A pilot declared an emergency that was intercepted by the OPS officer. He called AIROPS and ordered a course of action be taken that was wrong, dead wrong! I questioned him on his directions, and all hell broke loose, resulting in his ordering me to implement his decision. I said "Aye, Aye Sir" and commenced to put out his directions. Immediately, I was deluged with questions about what kind of Idiot was I, ordering such a stupid solution. I was informed that the solution I had ordered would most certainly result in the loss of the aircraft, and maybe the pilot. I had shared this same opinion with the OPS officer earlier when he exploded. Fortunately, everyone disobeyed the order I had made, and the aircraft's problem was solved resulting in a safe recovery.

After flight operations were complete for the night, I discussed this situation with Tom. He had similar experience with this officer in the past. We decided that in the future when the operations officer would call with instructions we would simply tell him "AYE, AYE SIR!", then completely disregard everything he said, then solve the problem as we saw fit. As situations arrived, he continued to call, we would answer "AYE, AYE SIR!", and forget about what he said. This worked. For the next three months of pre-deployment operations and nine months of combat operations in Southeast Asia we disregarded what he said. Not once did he realize what we were doing. Had Tom or I made a bum decision resulting in the loss of an aircraft or pilot, we could have been court-martialed. We never lost a plane!

DONALD L HOWE

OOPS!

Weather is the one factor that plagues airmen. It affected the Wright brothers just as much as it affects the launch and recovery of spacecraft. As men, we know a lot about the weather. We talk about it in almost every casual conversation. We watch with horror as a tornado rips a town apart. We make attempts at predicting it. But, NO ONE knows how to control it.

Air operations from an aircraft carrier are very similar to those from a land base. There are however, several major exceptions. On an aircraft carrier, the Captain can always point the ship into the wind, thus carrier pilots don't usually have to worry about crosswinds. The Captain can also jack up the power on the boat and create his own wind, if conditions so dictate. This is both an advantage and sometimes a disadvantage. It takes some practice trying to land on something that is continually trying to get away from you. Still, it is a solvable problem. Poor visibility, rain and fog are problems all aviators face and are not much different on a carrier. Catapult launches and arrested landings are unique to the carrier operation, but the basic takeoff and landing procedures still apply. The one major factor a carrier pilot faces is caused by the swells of the sea. The PITCHING DECK!

It's hard to believe that a ship so big could possible be affected by the swells in the sea. That is, until you see the size of some of the swells! During one passage across the Pacific, the aircraft had to be moved from the bow of the Hawk because green water was coming over the flight deck. That's seventy-two feet above the normal water line! A pitching deck can occur with much smaller swells.

During the night CARQUAL phase, the Hawk experienced heavy weather. No matter what the Captain did with the ship, we ended up with a pitching deck. A pitching deck is when the stern of the ship, or landing point, is going up and down because of the action of the sea. This particular night the deck was pitching up and down sixteen feet. Since the ship is semi-rigid, the bow is also going up and down, so care must be taken when an aircraft is catapulted off the ship that it isn't shot off into the water. This can easily be controlled by the catapult officer, who holds the firing of the cat until the precise moment. Aircraft landing have a much bigger problem.

The Hawk was equipped with a closed-circuit television camera positioned at the intended point of touchdown on the carrier deck. This camera pointed exactly up the glide slope, equipped with superimposed crosshairs. On a calm night (or day), when a plane intercepted the glide slope it appeared on the screen as a dot, or a light, usually at the intersection of the crosshairs. As it came closer the image grew until it was recognizable as an aircraft, then continually increased in size until it filled the entire screen, then disappeared when it touched down. When a pitching deck condition existed, the aircraft on the glide slope camera appeared to be going up and down through the glide slope in a serpentine action. It was, of course, the ship moving up and down, with the aircraft closing. The Hawk also had a standard television camera, operated by a cameraman that attempted to film the flight deck operations. The engineer controlling what went out into the ship's TV system would track the approaching aircraft on the glide slope camera until the point of touchdown, then immediately switch to the standard camera to watch the landing aircraft's TRAP and rollout. If aircraft were also being launched, an occasional CAT shot was aired. Thus, those of us who were buried in the bowels of the ship that had a vital interest into what was going on could keep up to date, and keep a good mental picture of the operation.

The LSO stands at the very end corner of the ship, in front of the mirror, as viewed by an approaching pilot. The LSO trains for months to learn to "feel" if an approaching aircraft can make a safe TRAP. He is the final clearance authority for landing, and causes a set of green lights to flash and calls "CUT, CUT" on the radio, if he feels the aircraft can TRAP safely. If he feels the aircraft should go around, for any reason, he flashes a set of red lights, fires a flare, and calls "Wave off, Wave off" on the radio. The LSO has a particular responsibility during pitching deck conditions in that he must also make sure the aircraft's landing will be in sync with the ship's deck movement.

On the night of the sixteen-foot pitching deck, there were several F4 Phantoms in the landing pattern. The pilot of one of these aircraft had made several landings previously and was on approach for his last CARQUAL landing. Intercepting final approach, the pilot called the ball inbound. The Phantom first appeared as a dot of light, going up and down thru the glide slope. A good approach, everything looked normal. At the CUT position the LSO gave the CUT signal and the aircraft made its landing transition. Just as the aircraft neared the point of touchdown, the ship lurched upward. The Phantom caught a wire, and landed very hard, driving the landing gear struts up through the wings in the process.

As the aircraft came to a stop, it exploded into a huge fireball. Fuel from the wing tanks, ruptured by the landing gear struts, spilled over the flight deck. For a few seconds after the explosion and initial fireball, the fire subsided. The wind across the flight deck kept the fire toward the rear of the plane. This allowed the pilot and radar officer to blow the canopy off the craft and scamper forward to safety. No sooner had the crew cleared the front of the plane when it exploded again into a large fireball equally as large as the first.

Damage control on the Hawk was practiced continually, and this practice paid off. The fire crew rallied and within seconds the wreckage was being foamed and the fire extinguished. Within minutes the hot wreckage was placed upon a long pallet and removed to a safe place, clearing the runway for further operations. The pilots were escorted to sick bay by members of the flight deck rescue team. They were treated for minor flash burns and released.

When the crash occurred, I ordered CATCC to take the other birds in the CARQUAL pattern up to a higher altitude (where they consumed less fuel), and to hold them until we got the go ahead. The Captain and CAG consulted and decided to continue the CARQUALS. When the deck was cleared we brought the birds back down and went about the business at hand.

The next day I inspected the remains of the ill-fated Phantom that had subsequently been moved onto the hangar deck. All that was left of that 50,000-pound aircraft was a pile of now cooled molten metal about the size of an automobile. This was the way of carrier operations. One second everything was fine. The next, all hell would break loose.

RIDING THE ROLLER COASTER

Jet pilots are usually energetic young men who jump at the chance of doing something a little different, especially if it gives them a chance to show off a bit. The pilots in the Hawk's air wing were not any different.

Occasionally during the CARQUAL phase everything went right, allowing the pilot to complete his qualification and have a little time and fuel left over. The pilot can use this time to bore holes in the sky, go check out the nearest island, even buzz the beach if he is close enough. If two pilots find themselves in this situation at the same time they can go dogfighting for a spell. This extra flight time didn't cost the government anything because the excess fuel not burned during the hop would be dumped to get the aircraft weight down to the maximum allowable for landing. Thus, the pilot is free to do whatever he wants, within reason, as long as it is safe.

After completing his qualification landings, one F4 Phantom jockey decided he would like to make a high-speed pass by the ship. The Phantom is a fast airplane. A high-speed pass would be very impressive to those on the ship.

After completing the pass, the pilot would proceed back to his land base, completing the mission.

The AIR BOSS was controlling the landing pattern and had no objections to the pass as long as it didn't interfere with the other birds. A course was decided upon that would allow this fledgling pilot to make his pass. He maneuvered his aircraft to the agreed starting position and proceeded inbound.

Now the Phantom is a good airplane, but it is still a flying machine, and most flying machines have certain quirks about them that seem to exhibit themselves at the most inopportune time. Experienced pilots know most of the quirks about the plane they are flying and try to avoid the conditions that bring them about. These same pilots then brief the inexperienced pilots about these quirks, in an attempt to share their knowledge and keep some youngster from busting his butt over a stupid thing. Thus, our young jet throttle jockey had been briefed, but had never experienced what was about to happen.

The Phantom pilot started his run ahead of and on a course opposite that of the ship, intending on dropping down to and maintaining about 100 feet altitude as he passed by the ship. Once he was established inbound, the pilot activated his afterburners and accelerated his craft to a speed just under the speed of sound, about 650 knots. When the aircraft was about one-fourth mile in front of the ship it went into an uncontrolled porpoising maneuver, oscillating first up, then down. No one quite knows why the Phantom does this, or at least they couldn't explain it to me. It has something to do with the pilot applying corrective control out of phase with the oscillations, aggravating the situation instead of correcting it. If the oscillations continued they became more pronounced making the amplitude greater and greater. If the pilot has enough altitude they can recover from it, but at 100 feet?

The aircraft completed one full oscillation, maybe two (it was hard to tell). When the plane was at the top of its last oscillation at about 300 feet, the pilot and the radar officer wisely decided to exit the now out of control aircraft and activated their rocket powered ejection seats or "punched out". The aircraft continued over the top along its ill-fated flight path crashing nose down into the water.

It was MOST impressive to those of us on the ship, just not quite what the pilot had planned.

The AIRBOSS directed the ships rescue helicopter to the downed pilot and radar officer. The helicopter, called the "HOOKIE", was always airborne with the crew ready to perform their life saving maneuvers during all flight operations. The HOOKIE located the downed airmen and approached them slowly, allowing them to get out of and clear of their parachute shroud lines. The downwash from the helicopter could entangle an airman downed in the water, and actually drag him under the surface. When the downed pilots were clear the HOOKIE lifted them aboard and returned to them to the ship. After a few minutes both were safely aboard the Hawk, showing only minor scrapes and bruises caused by their high-speed ejection.

As is the case in accidents of this nature, a lot of finger pointing and blame circled around the ship, mostly by those who did not understand the quirks that aircraft have. Officially, the young lad got his hands slapped, but let the record show that he actually did everything right. It was a common practice for pilots to make high-speed passes. He had obtained the proper clearance and followed the prescribed course. When the plane went into the porpoise he did the right thing to eject himself and the radar officer. Trying to save the craft would most likely proved fatal to both of them because it was beyond control at that point anyway. The quirk of the Phantom really was the culprit. No one knew when the quirk would strike again.

There is a saying in aviation circles that goes like this:

"There are old pilots, and there are bold pilots, but there are no old, bold pilots."

This young Phantom jockey and his radar officer luckily walked away from this accident a little older, but a lot less bold, as they came to understand how carrier aviation can change from sweet to sour in a split second. It is said that all pilots live near the edge. Tailhookers live just a little closer.

NOSE OVER

When flying, a pilot has to be mentally ahead of his aircraft from the time he gets into it, throughout the flight, and until he secures it in the chocks after landing. Although this is a simple concept, it is sometimes forgotten by pilots, usually to their own detriment.

During one session of CARQUALS an A4 Skyhawk from the Naval Test center at Patuxant River, Maryland came aboard to qualify the pilot and to test some equipment aboard the specially equipped aircraft. The plan was for the pilot to make one TRAP aboard, be briefed by the LSO, then go back out for the remainder of his qualification landings. After he had qualified he would complete the remainder of his equipment testing mission and be on his way. Now pilots assigned to Patuxant River were the "cream of the crop" as pilots go. They were very experienced, proven and had successfully attended "Test Pilot School". The original Astronauts were chosen from their ranks.

It was late in the morning and a visual CARQUAL landing pattern was in progress. The weather was clear, with excellent visibility and the deck reasonably stable, with a very slight rolling motion. Conditions were ideal. The Skyhawk arrived as planned and checked in with the AIRBOSS. He was instructed to join the pattern, then control was passed to the LSO. The pilot made a near-perfect approach and TRAP. Everything looked great. After release from the arresting cable, the flight deck crew took over and directed the pilot to taxi over onto the forward elevator where he would be taken down and prepared for the next launch. The pilot taxied over onto the elevator, stopped his plane, set his parking brake and shut down the engine.

The elevator was lowered. About the time it reached the hangar deck, the ship rolled slightly to the right and the Skyhawk, with pilot aboard, simply rolled off the elevator into the water.

It seems that a design condition existed with the Skyhawk that if the brakes and parking brakes were not set in the correct sequence during engine shutdown and the subsequent loss of main system hydraulic pressure, the brake system locks up somewhere in the middle and NO brakes are actually set. The pilot had momentarily forgotten this condition, and thought he had secured the plane when he hadn't. The ship's crew was at fault for not chocking the wheels before the aircraft power was shut down. The crew however, was not used to handling Skyhawk aircraft, as there were none normally aboard the Hawk.

The Skyhawk did not sink immediately. The pilot climbed out of the cockpit and sat on top the plane waiting for the rescue helicopter. The rescue helicopter, affectionately called the "HOOKIE", picked up the pilot without further incident and returned him to the ship. The pilot was unhurt. He was however, embarrassed, frustrated, and now having to return home and explain this to his superiors. To complicate matters, this was no ordinary Skyhawk. It was loaded with millions of dollars worth of prototype electronics, all lost when the craft sank. The pilot knew of the hydraulic/brake system condition but momentarily forgot. He had literally forgotten to "fly" the plane all the way to the chocks.

Not long after the Skyhawk plunge, a second incident occurred where the pilot forgot to continually "fly" his aircraft. An F4 Phantom was preparing to launch off the waist CAT during an early evening CARQUAL session. The pilot had completed his take off checklist, and when directed by the flight deck crew taxied up onto the catapult into the launch position. At this point the catapult crew hooked up the plane to the catapult. The pilot then applied full power, fired the afterburners and saluted the catapult Officer, signaling his readiness for launch. The Catapult Officer visually checked the aircraft, the catapult and general area. After receiving a thumbs-up from the petty officer monitoring the catapult instruments and determining all was ready the catapult officer gave the firing signal and the CAT crew commenced firing.

Normal procedure at this point would be for the pilot to hold the control stick all the way back into his lap and brace himself for the CAT shot. Holding the control stick all the way back positions the aircraft's stabilator (horizontal tail control surface) in the full nose up position, required by the Phantom to catapult launch. For one slight moment, the pilot relaxed his grip on the stick allowing the aircraft's stabilator to come out of the full up position. The catapult officer noticed the stabilator move out of position at the same time the pilot caught his error and corrected, but too late for either to stop the CAT shot.

When the CAT fires, the aircraft goes! It goes regardless of the aircraft's condition. It goes whether the pilot is ready or not. The pilot could have his wheel brakes locked and it wouldn't make any difference. When the CAT fires, the aircraft goes!

The Phantom was catapulted off the deck and immediately pitched about thirty degrees nose down. As the nose fell toward the water the radar officer ejected. His rocket-powered ejection seat carried him in a trajectory over the bow of the ship and into the water on the right side.

Everyone waited for the pilot's ejection and the plane to crash! Nothing happened.

After what seemed like an eternity, out in front of the ship came the Phantom! It was nose high with the tail at water level, blowing two large troughs in the water with its afterburners. The aircraft accelerated remaining at water level for about one half mile. It was then able to commence a climb to a safe altitude. The pilot was then able to fly his craft, less the cockpit canopy, back to a land base for repairs.

Observing the ejection, the HOOKIE crew quickly moved into position, picked up the radar officer and returned him to the ship, unharmed. The Phantom configuration allows the radar officer to eject without automatically ejecting the pilot. The reverse is not true. If the pilot were to eject, the radar officer automatically goes too.

No one knows why the pilot relaxed his grip on the control stick. Even the pilot didn't realize he had done it. When the pilot did realize his error he repositioned the stick in just the right split second of time to get the aircraft flying in the correct attitude before it hit the water. The tail may even have struck the water assisting in the recovery, no one knows. What is known is that all aircraft have to be flown from "chock to chock". A relaxation of this rule almost always brings sudden, irreversible and sometimes fatal consequences.

HAWAII

There is never enough time to get all the practice done before the ship has to deploy. Departing home port was also a time of sorrow, with everyone trying to be brave and upbeat, but with the underlying knowledge that we would be apart from wives and children for at least nine months. This was also a cruise taking us into combat during the Vietnam conflict. For an unknown few it would be a final good-bye. Nobody wanted to think about that!

Once underway, and everyone being in the same boat, things were not as bad. In AIROPS our primary responsibility was to set up an alert watch, with two Phantoms parked on the waist CATS and their pilots ready to launch in their ready rooms. We also had an A3 tanker plane and crew on a 30-minute alert. These watches were spread around requiring only one in four of our personnel actually working. Major BOREDOM ensued. A movie theater was set up in AIROPS, showing three or four features a day of 1945 vintage or earlier films. We usually had between twenty or thirty takers, just to pass the time. Walking and running the flight deck also became popular, along with two or three scratch football games. Normally the hangar deck could be used for basketball, but it was full of aircraft, and other stuff during the "Transpac" (Pacific Ocean crossing).

Four days out of San Diego we began flight operations, this time to train for precision bombing at the Kaahoolawe bombing range. Our operations here were set up to simulate operations on Yankee station, in the Tonkin Gulf where we were destined. We were close enough to suitable landing fields in the Hawaiian Islands in case a BINGO was required. For the most part our operations were routine, with only a few minor emergencies. This gave us all a chance to hone our skills to a fine edge. We operated in this mode for three days then headed into Pearl Harbor.

We were in port for two days. During this time the ship had to have a major repair accomplished, to correct a problem that had developed in the system that makes fresh water from salt water. In AIROPS we had a day's work planning for the next few days flight operations when we left Pearl Harbor, but almost everyone managed to get one day "on the beach".

As the Hawk pulled up to the dock, it was interesting to note a sweet young stewardess waiting. She was there to meet one of the ship's senior officers, who just happened to be the first person off the ship. It was both amusing and sad, as just a few weeks earlier we had met this man's wife, and she was a very nice lady and didn't deserve being treated this way. It certainly was not a smart thing to wander like an alley cat for several reasons. Not the least of these reasons was the "grape vine" among the wives left behind. There were those aboard the ship that minded their own business, and those who wrote home about all that happened, or allegedly happened. It was not uncommon for us to hear from home of things that happened on the ship only one week earlier. This officer's antics were talked about among the crew for weeks to come.

The installation of the ship's equipment took an extra day, so everyone that wanted to go ashore had at least one day on Oahu. When leaving port it was announced that the ship's water system now had a three times greater capacity to make fresh water, and that "Water Hours" were not anticipated. What that really meant was that everyone could take a "Navy Shower", once a day if they desired. This was welcomed because operations off the coast of Southeast Asia was always hot, regardless of the time of year. A special assist for AIROPS was the installation also increased the capacity of the "Chilled water" system. Chilled water was vital in maintaining the temperature of the radar equipment at an operational level, thus allowing us to control aircraft. It also kept our working spaces cool, which was very welcome.

Almost as soon as we left port and cleared the channel into Pearl Harbor we started flight operations. The weather was good but we encountered large swells almost immediately, and had to operate with a pitching deck. With only two days to operate before we would be out of range of any suitable BINGO fields, we made the most of it.

Mid-afternoon of the first day out we saw a different kind of incident. An A7 Corsair returning from a practice bombing mission was making a visual approach for a landing. The pilot made a good approach and touchdown, but did not catch a wire. He went around and tried a second time. Again, a good approach and touchdown right where he should be but without a TRAP. The AIRBOSS sent the A7 up to altitude for a visual inspection by his wingman. It was discovered that the aircraft had lost its hook! The hook shaft was there but the hook was missing.

There were two alternative courses of action. We could take the plane aboard into the "BARRICADE" or send it back to Barbers Point Naval Air Station, on Oahu, for repairs. Using the barricade often had less than optimum results in that some damage to the aircraft almost always occurred. The barricade was, after all, nothing more than a series of Nylon straps woven together to make a huge net that was strung across the runway. The aircraft would land the same as an arrested landing, then be stopped as it rolled into the net. The drawback of sending the plane ashore was that we were rapidly leaving the area, and if the aircraft could not be repaired immediately, it would have to be left behind. The Corsair did not have the range to fly from Hawaii to the Philippines or Japan without a tanker enroute. It was possible for the plane to fly to Midway Island, refuel and meet a tanker from the Hawk west of Midway, then both aircraft return to the ship. It was decided to send the Corsair back to Barbers point.

The AIRBOSS gave the Corsair his BINGO signal, and he motored off to Barbers point. Parts were available and he was back a few hours later making a successful TRAP.

Flight operations for the next day were cancelled because of the swells. The seas were humongous. The flight deck had to move the aircraft normally tied down on the bow of the ship back a couple hundred feet because of the green water coming over the bow. This was not uncommon for smaller ships, like a destroyer, or even a cruiser, but the Hawk's flight deck was seventy feet above the water! No one even measured how much the deck was pitching. It was even difficult to walk down a passageway without being slammed against the walls. The ship felt more like a destroyer than an aircraft carrier. Many of the crew were turning green with seasickness, rare on a ship the size of the Hawk. Our feelings went out to those aboard the two destroyers sailing with us. They were being turned everyway but loose.

The heavy swells lasted about three days. We were all overjoyed to sail into more calm waters. The Captain was also overjoyed because he could now increase the ship's speed and make up time for what had been lost in port and in the heavy swells. At this point we were two days behind.

The next week was probably the hardest time for the married members of the crew. We were away from home long enough for it to sink in that we were going to be away for a very long time. There was also very little to do, allowing minds to wander and dwell on the negative side of things. For everyone there was the uncertainty of going into war, especially for the pilots and flight crewmembers who had not been there before. Those who had work to do were the lucky ones. For the rest of us, the time dragged by.

DONALD L HOWE

IN THE MIDDLE OF NOWHERE

The Soviet Union had some very long-range aircraft capable of conducting operations in the South Pacific Ocean. When we came into this area our defensive posture upgraded to meet the potential threat.

Our alert posture now included two F4 phantoms sitting on the waist CATS with pilots and radar officers aboard, ready to start and launch. An A3 Skywarrior was also held in a 30-minute alert status. In AIROPS we were manned with about half our crew, a minimum to conduct flight operations. Boredom showed its ugly face again but this time we excluded the AIROPS theater and suffered through.

We didn't have long to wait. Several days out of Pearl Harbor we were to be visited. We were in international waters in an area open to all. The Soviets had as much right to be there as did we, thus all either force would probably do is look at each other and take pictures. However, we were a military force engaged in hostilities with allies of the Soviets. Even though the probability was great that all they would do was look, we couldn't bet our future on it.

CIC reported an incoming contact and we scrambled the Phantoms. We also launched an A3 Tanker. Two additional Phantoms were put into the ready position. The Phantoms proceeded to intercept the incoming contact. It turned out to be a commercial airliner that was not properly identifying itself. The F4's and the tanker flew around for a while then returned to the ship and TRAPPED without incident. It was a good exercise.

The next day it was the same scenario. The ready phantoms were launched, checked out the target finding it to be a friendly airliner, then returned to TRAP. The day following, same. same.

Just when we thought we would spend the entire Transpac chasing unidentified airliners, the soviets came. We dutifully launched the phantoms but held the tanker in ready along with two other F4'S. This time we hit pay dirt and the intercepting Phantoms positively identified the incoming target as a Soviet. We then launched the tanker and the other two Phantoms.

The soviet aircraft was proceeding directly toward the Hawk. This in itself was not an aggressive act, but it did bring a lot of tension into the situation.

As was the procedure, our Phantoms trailed behind and to one side, in a firing position. This was done just in case the intruding aircraft did something that looked hostile, like opening their bomb-bay doors, or locking onto the ship with fire control radar. Attempts at radio contact were made on the universal guard frequency with no response. The intruding aircraft continued inbound. The tension mounted.

When the soviet aircraft was about thirty miles out it began a descent so as to pass over the ship at a lower altitude. The Phantoms continued to track the aircraft inbound, until when at 20 miles, they activated their missile lock-on radar. The Soviet plane made an immediate turn of a few degrees so as not to pass directly over the Hawk, a sign of non-hostility, The Phantoms and the ships own missile radar continued to track the plane until it passed ahead of the ship, then made a gentle turn to come around for a photo pass.

The large Soviet plane made one pass on a heading against that of the ship, made a 180 degree turn and made a second pass down the other side of the ship on a parallel heading. Throughout all the intruder's passes, the two Phantoms maintained a firing position. The soviet craft then made a gentle turn to the right and began a climb heading away from the ship on a northerly heading. When the Soviet aircraft was about 20 miles away from the ship, the Phantoms secured their missile control radars, but continued to track the intruders until they were over 100 miles away and opening.

People are people whether they be Russian or U.S. Both crews seemed to enjoy the encounter, as everyone waved to each other. It seems the Soviets just wanted to keep track of what we were sending into the war effort, and let us know that they had the capability to operate where we were. We wanted to let the Soviets know that we could and would defend ourselves if they wanted to engage in any hanky-panky along the way. Both we and the Soviets knew that had they made the slightest act of aggression they would have been shot out of the sky. Thus, they just made a friendly photo pass, something we did to them with our patrol aircraft all the time.

After the Phantoms broke off their encounter with the Soviet plane we gave them fuel. After flying around for a while all five aircraft returned for successful and uneventful TRAPS. We continued on our way to Southeast Asia, keeping our ready watch set, trying to combat the boredom. This was our only encounter with the Soviets.

FIRE! FIRE! FIRE!

Drills and practice make one very proficient at doing necessary jobs. We all have certain things that have to be done. Often times we don't want to do the deed assigned, but it is part of our job, so we do it. No one particularly wanted to practice the fire drills that were held at least daily, but it was one of those necessary rituals that had to be done, so we all accepted.

The fire drill was announced over the ship's public address system with a dinging of a bell, followed by the words: "This is a drill! This is a drill! FIRE! FIRE! FIRE! There is a fire on the . . ." The location was announced and all hands directed to remain clear while the fire party proceeded to the fire or their fire station, as applicable. The fire party takes priority over all other activities, and if you didn't get out of their way they went right over or through you. There was good reason for their actions. Time was of the essence. The ships crew was organized into fire fighting squads that had attended damage control schools. These crews were normally assigned in the areas where they worked or berthed such that all of the ship was covered. This was a "second job" so to speak, in that all of the people had primary jobs they would leave in the event of a fire, or drill. Obviously, there were some persons that were assigned to critical jobs that were never assigned to a fire party. The Air controllers in CATCC were in that category, as were those driving the ship and certain of the engineers that kept the boat running.

With over 5500 personnel, over 100 aircraft, with equipment to sustain a 9-month deployment coupled with fuel and ordnance aboard, it was not uncommon to have a real fire once in a while. Fire, no matter how small, was never treated lightly. Small fires aboard a ship can rapidly develop into very large fires, thus even the smallest fire was treated with the whole regalia. The down side to all of this is that the fires or fire drills happened with such frequency that one would sometimes become complacent about the whole thing. I think many of us were at that state the night this incident occurred.

"FIRE! FIRE! FIRE! There is a fire in the main engine room. All hands remain clear . . ." The fire signal rang out loud and clear. It was not a drill! Fire in the main engine room was not a good sign. "GENERAL QUARTERS! GENERAL-QUARTERS! All hands man your battle stations . . ." The transmission rang out loud and clear almost immediately after the fire signal had been sent. This must really be serious. General Quarters always activates everyone on the ship, and is designed to take the ship to its most battle-ready state in a minimum amount of time. We accounted for everyone and reported to the bridge, "AIROPS Manned and Ready!"

At this point, while waiting for orders to do something, conjecture as to what may be the problem runs rampant. Were we under attack? Not too likely. Was the ship burning in the main engine room, about to burn through into the fuel tanks or the magazines? Possible, but again, not too likely. Had there been some kind of accident? General Quarters may be called, but the reason was never given. While our curiosity was going bananas, we did NOT call the bridge and ask what was going on. The bridge was the main control point of the ship, and even though damage control and fire-fighting were controlled from a different location, it was not prudent to bother the bridge. Instead, I called the flight deck control station. They said that something had blown up in the engine room, they thought. Obviously, they didn't know any more than I, so we waited patiently to find out what was happening.

We didn't have long to wait. After about ten minutes, the bridge secured General Quarters and the fire call was cancelled a few minutes after that. It seems that someone was using some diesel fuel to clean a piece of equipment. The bucket of fuel was accidentally spilled and ignited, filling the main engine room with smoke. The smoke was so thick that the officer on duty over-reacted. Not knowing the source or cause of the smoke, and seeing the denseness of it, he reacted as though a major fire was in the making. Always better to be more precautious than sorry.

The very next day the ship's TV newscast reported a fire aboard a sister carrier that had developed into major proportions, causing explosions killing a number of men and destroying several levels of the ship, rendering it out of action until repairs could be made. We all took the fire drills a little more seriously after that.

DONALD L HOWE

BACK IN THE SADDLE AGAIN!

Intuition is a funny thing. I can't explain why I had reservations about launching a whole bunch of aircraft, it was just there. It was the second launch on Yankee Station after a long training period. Everyone including the captain wanted to make a good impression on our first day of operations. Everyone except me, AIROPS, at least that is how it seemed.

The weather was not very good. The current visibility was okay, but the temperature / dew point spread was very low, it was late afternoon, and the wind, what little there was of it, was varying from all directions. A classic setup for fog, a pilot's worst enemy. The Captain was having to make the wind over the flight deck for our launch and recovery, and our course was taking us directly toward Hanoi.

The ship's strike center, who assigned all combat missions, wanted to launch a few extra birds, again to make a good impression. I said no, because the launch already had fourteen aircraft. Fourteen aircraft was the maximum CATCC could comfortably handle, in case we got into an instrument recovery situation. Fourteen aircraft seemed low to the people in strike center when would normally launch twenty during daylight visual operations. They were new, and didn't have a feel for changing conditions on Yankee station. They were also crafty enough to immediately call the Captain. The Captain then called me, informing me that the weather wasn't that bad, and expressed his desire to launch the extra birds. I presented my case, but he reminded me that I couldn't see outside (which was true), and that he felt it would be okay. When the captain speaks, everybody listens, so who was I to object? The launch ended up with 24 birds; six F4 Phantoms, four A6 Intruders, ten A7 Corsairs, two A5 Vigilantes, one A3 Skywarrior tanker, and one E-2 Hawkeye airborne CIC.

The normal cycle on Yankee Station lasted one hour and forty-five minutes from launch to launch. Each cycle consisted of a launch of outgoing aircraft and a recovery of returning planes. The launch normally started ten minutes before the recovery, then continued off the bow CATS until complete. Theoretically, one bird can be launched every fifteen seconds. In practice it averaged about one bird every 40 seconds. When the launch spilled over into the recovery time, clearing and keeping the runway clear became a major problem. It was further compounded when there were still a large number of birds to launch. This launch went very well in spite of the large number of birds, and so did the subsequent recovery.

As the recovery proceeded and was near complete, the ship began steaming into intermittent light fog. This was not yet a problem because the aircraft were operating visual and could still see the ship. All the planes landed safely until the last one, an E-2 Hawkeye. When the Pilot lined up he was not quite heading down the runway, moving from right to left. He touched down, caught a wire, and was brought to a stop, but not before he ran out of runway on the left side. The left main wheel went over the side into the catwalk.

As carrier accidents go, this was not serious. No one was hurt, and the plane received minimal damage. The problem was the aircraft was stuck there, and had to be removed before the flight deck crew could re-spot aircraft for the next launch and recovery. In the mean time, the temperature dropped and the weather worsened. Even though the ship had reversed course, the fog thickened and became very heavy.

It was obvious to me that major delays were approaching. Delay means time, and time to AIROPS means fuel being used. Fuel at this point was a finite commodity. When fuel ran out, the pilots couldn't just stop and wait for the tanker. With a major delay and limited giveaway fuel airborne, I could see MANY planes coming to a low fuel state condition. I ordered my controllers and the CIC people to contact all the birds, having them to maximum conserve their fuel.

Clearing the flight deck proved more of a problem than anyone expected. It also took much more time than we really had. The next launch had to be cancelled because the previously recovered birds could not be re-spotted. The scheduled recovery slipped by thirty minutes, then forty. Finally, when the AIR BOSS felt confident his crew could have the flight deck ready, we were given a time to start recovering the twenty-four airborne aircraft. The AIR BOSS also informed me that the weather was really bad, that he couldn't even see the stern of the ship. I was then called by the Captain who confirmed what the AIR BOSS had said. The Captain couldn't see the bow of the ship from the bridge. We are supposed to land aircraft in this? For the most part, you have to see the ship to land on it! I wanted to call everyone and say "I told you so!", but I didn't have time. AIROPS & CATCC had to try, to do the best we could.

Since we needed extra fuel in the air, a plan was devised to launch an A3 tanker, then start the recovery. It was a good plan, but the Skywarrior we were to launch developed a mechanical problem, and could not go. In a normal recovery with twelve to fourteen aircraft, the birds were all started down from marshal at the same time. AS each aircraft started its penetration, the bird above was cleared to descend to the first aircraft's altitude. With so many birds to recover, CATCC & I agreed to break the recovery up into three groups, keeping the second and third groups at altitude as long as possible to conserve their fuel. Normally the phantoms and Vigilantes were brought down first because they were the heavy fuel users. The exception to this procedure was the BARCAP or Barrier combat Air patrol. The BARCAP Phantoms were the ship's own defense, and normally were relieved by other Phantoms before returning for recovery & thus arrived later. There were no launching Phantoms, so the returning BARCAP remained on station as long as possible before returning.

One piece of equipment installed on the ship during the training period was the Automatic Carrier Landing System (ACLS). Theoretically, an aircraft on approach could "couple" with the ship's ACLS and. the "black boxes" or electronics would do the rest, bringing the aircraft in to a TRAP, hands off. This procedure was called an "AUTOMATIC APPROACH". This system was designed for the very situation the Hawk was in. There was only one problem. Only the Intruders and a few Corsairs had the hardware installed in their aircraft, and could utilize the system. We were grateful for whatever we could get.

All the aircraft in the first recovery group were or would be below BINGO fuel state when they reached the BALL. Knowing this we positioned the A3 tanker where they could "HAWK" (all caps) the landing planes that wouldn't have enough fuel to make another approach. "HAWKING" was to have the tanker in a position above and in front of the landing aircraft so that when a BOLTER or MISSED APPROACH was made all the pilot had to do was pull up, plug in, and take fuel from the tanker. Thus the recovery began.

The first two Phantoms made their approaches to minimums, initiated missed approaches, and never saw the ship even though they flew right over it at 100 feet altitude. They were put into the downwind pattern for another approach. BY some miracle, the third aircraft, a Vigilante, saw the ship in a break in the fog, and TRAPPED successfully. The fourth aircraft, another Vigilante at low fuel state, completed his approach and never saw the ship. The A3 tanker was in HAWKING position, enabling the Vigilante to pop up and take on fuel. We gave him 2500 pounds, about half of our "GIVEAWAY FUEL", enough for him to make two more approaches. The fifth approach was the first Phantom to make an approach and wave-off. Again, a small hole opened up and this time he was able to TRAP successfully. Approach numbers six and seven were A6 Intruders, both took automatic approaches and TRAPPED successfully, blind in the fog. The eighth approach was Phantom number two that had previously waved off. He never saw the ship, and went around again, with enough fuel for one more approach. Approach number nine was a Phantom that was at low fuel state on the ball. He didn't see the ship, and the A3 tanker was still tied up with the A5. We sent him away to join the tanker, to take the balance of the giveaway fuel. His wingman, approach number 10, was also at low fuel state, but was lucky. He saw the BALL (not the ship) and TRAPPED successfully. Approach number 11 was phantom number two again. This time he made it aboard.

The second group of aircraft had departed Marshal and were about five minutes out. Their updated fuel states indicated they were also below BINGO fuel, and would have to recover. Group number three were at BINGO fuel, at altitude. They would certainly be below BINGO fuel if I held them further. I personally came up on their radio frequency and ordered them to divert to Danang, about 125 miles away. This group consisted of two Phantoms and six Corsairs. All of the birds acknowledged except two Corsairs. They were already below BINGO state. I ordered them to remain overhead, informing them we would try to send the tanker, and if they ran out fuel before we could get to them, to call the ship then "PUNCH OUT" (Pilot's eject themselves from the aircraft). We would then pick them up with the helicopter.

The Vigilante from the first group had completed taking fuel from the tanker and returned as approach number 12, to successfully TRAP. This left a lone Phantom, from the first group, who was tanking, yet to recover. Group two birds were now on final approach. Approach number 13 was a Corsair that was ACLS equipped, but the pilot had never performed an AUTOMATIC approach. He knew the procedure, coupled as directed by the final controller, and trapped successfully, in the blind. WHAT FAITH! Approach number 14 was a Corsair, who never saw the ship. Approach number 15 was an Intruder equipped for ACLS, but his ACLS equipment was not functioning, and he had to shoot a manual approach. Again, a break in the fog, and he made it in.

I then received a call from the flight leader of the six aircraft I had diverted to Danang. He had reported in to Danang Approach Control and been informed he would be number seventeen in the EMERGENCY approach pattern into Danang. The expected approach time he was given was twenty minutes after he would run out of fuel. BIG DECISION TIME! These six aircraft did not have enough fuel to return to the Hawk and could not hold long enough to get into Danang! The tanker squadron skipper, who was monitoring this fiasco with me in AIROPS, suggested we send them to Thailand. Nakom Phanon was a small base used by forward air controllers, but it could handle our birds. I made the decision and transmitted: "99 PAWTUCKET, YOUR SIGNAL BINGO TO NAKOM PHANON". The birds acknowledged, and went their way.

About this time, I was notified by the AIR BOSS that the A3 tanker we wanted to launch earlier could now be launched. This would be about 24,000 pounds of giveaway fuel if we could get him up. I ordered the launch.

Approach number 16, an Intruder, was on short final making an AUTOMATIC approach, He trapped successfully. We launched the A3 tanker. I directed he go immediately to the two Corsairs orbiting overhead at low fuel state. Approach number 17 was the Phantom from group one that had to take on fuel. He never saw the ship. Approach number 18 was a Corsair, again, who never saw the ship.

As we got closer to the North Vietnamese coast, the weather gave us a break. What had been a fog layer raised into a low overcast. It was also getting dark, where lights could be seen at greater distances. Thus, approach number 19, a Corsair and approach number 20, a Skywarrior and our first tanker, both made it aboard. Approach numbers 21, 22 and 23 were the birds we had in the wave-off pattern and all made it aboard okay, but two of these aircraft would not have had enough fuel for another approach. Approach number 24 was the Hawkeye, sister to the aircraft that started the whole mess. They TRAPPED successfully.

When the last launched A3 tanker joined the two Corsairs orbiting overhead, one of them slipped in and immediately took fuel. In the Corsair the fuel gage reads accurately until it gets down to 300 pounds. At this point you may or may not have fuel left. As the tanker pulled along side, the plane's fuel gage had been at the 300-pound level for over a minute. Both Corsairs took on fuel. After refueling, all three aircraft returned making approach numbers 25, 26 and 27. We had caught all but six planes from group three, diverted to Nakom phanon. We had made 27 instrument approaches with 19 TRAPS. A normal flight would be a maximum of two hours and fifteen minutes. The last bird to trap, a Corsair, had been airborne three-and-one-half hours.

On a later launch we got the word through one of our aircraft that all six aircraft sent BINGO had landed safely at Nakom Phanon. We never found out until the pilots returned what the real story was. The first Phantom flamed out or ran out of fuel, just as he touched down. He rolled to a stop but could not clear the runway. He was able to pull to one side, allowing the second Phantom and the Corsairs to land. The second Phantom flamed out just after clearing the runway but had to be towed to its parking spot. Two of the Corsairs also landed safely, but flamed out prior to reaching the parking area. The other two landed without incident.

During the entire recovery I was so involved I never had a chance to call the Captain. After it was all over, I called. He was very gracious. I was very upset but tried to be civil. NO ONE ever questioned my intuition again.

BIG MOTHER TRUCKERS

Combat air operations unfortunately results in aircraft being shot down, or their just having problems resulting in an ejection over enemy territory. World War II pilots were pretty much on their own, having to escape and evade the enemy, receiving assistance from the underground. The Korean War saw the introduction of helicopters to make rescues of downed airmen. This was at best an art in its infancy. The Vietnam War developed helicopter rescues to a true art, and many downed pilots owe their lives to their success.

In addition to the Air Wing permanently assigned to the Hawk, we would also have the rescue helicopter detachment aboard during much of the time we were on Yankee station. The helicopters used by this detachment were many generations advanced from the choppers used in Korea. They were big, armor plated, jet powered, and had the range to make "in country" pickups. They were Navy birds, designed to operate off a carrier or other flat deck, being able to fold their rotors and be tucked away in a corner. A large corner, that is. Next to these helicopters our ship's rescue HOOKIE looked like a toy.

The call sign of this detachment was "BIG MOTHER". Thus, the detachment became known as the "BIG MOTHER TRUCKERS".

My introduction to the Big Mothers came the first night they flew aboard the Hawk. It was a visual recovery, just before dark. They were transferring from another carrier that was leaving Yankee station, and were to be aboard the Hawk for the next 30 days. The recovery was normal, and other than the usual bitching by the Flight Deck Officer wondering where he would put these four big helicopters, no one thought anything more about it.

We were preparing for our next launch of fixed wing aircraft when a strapping young pilot came into AIROPS. He wore a 45-caliber pistol on his right hip, and a flare gun on his left. He had a six-shooter stuck in his cartridge belt, with another in a shoulder harness. He was further equipped with two crossing bandoliers over his shoulders, stuffed full of ammunition. In addition to this armament he had a knife that would have done Jim Bowie proud strapped to his leg, and a ten-gallon hat. Except for his standard dark green flight suit underneath all this armament, he could have come straight from the Alamo! This gent boldly marched up in front of my console and announced his presence: "Hi! My name's TEX! I'm a Big Mother Trucker!"

Silence was the word, mainly because most of us in AIROPS were totally speechless. I didn't know if I should say "Hi!" or hide under the console. I didn't have to wait long. Almost involuntarily, the whole room burst into uncontrollable laughter, Tex included.

We welcomed Tex and his Big Mother Truckers aboard the Hawk. We thanked him for the work he did, all the while hoping that none of our pilots would have to use his services. We found out that Tex wore this costume while performing his mission, vowing that if he ever got shot down that he wouldn't go without a fight. If you met Tex on the street in downtown Dallas he would appear as any other clean-cut young man. From his appearance that night he could successfully take on the entire North Vietnamese army!

We used Tex and his compatriots several times, but fortunately not for pilots off the Hawk. The Big Mothers did have occasion to pick up several Air Force and Marine types, who were most grateful. These rescue missions never went in alone. They were always escorted by fighter and attack aircraft from our ship that provided close air support during the rescue, and a tanker for refueling after their return. My hat goes off to Tex and the Big Mother Truckers, and all the others including the Air Force JOLLY GREEN GIANTS, who flew their choppers in at tree top level amidst hostile fire much of the way and plucked our downed airmen away from the enemy. Not all of them made it back.

Not many of the pilots had the flamboyance of Tex and the Big Mother Truckers. But, they all had the determination to do the best and the most they could. Not a day passed without several attack pilots stopping by AIROPS asking to be added to the AIR PLAN with an extra flight. Whenever an extra mission developed there were always numerous volunteers, ready to do the job. This was typical of all the young pilots, in total contrast to their college counterparts who were demonstrating and protesting the entire war. It was obvious that these demonstrating young people had no idea of what was happening in Vietnam. Had they witnessed some of the atrocities performed by the Viet Cong on the Vietnamese people, they may have changed their tune.

THE HAWK BAND

Flight operations aboard the Hawk ran for twelve hours. Add another two hours before and two hours after and you had the standard working day. In spite of the sixteen plus hours on the job, there was always time and a definite need for diversion. For some this came in the form of the HAWK BAND.

The Hawk Band was not made up of musicians or even from anyone professing musical talent. It was just a bunch of guys having a good time, trying to relax. The "musical instruments" consisted of whatever could be assembled to make some kind of noise that could be blended into all the other noise emitting from the rest of the group. They had a base made from a washtub and a string hooked to a broomstick, a "sweet potato", comb & tissue, ukulele, washboard, banjo, and a few other "instruments" that are beyond description. Surprisingly enough, they sounded pretty good! Some even said they sounded better after a few drinks, but I'm not sure who was doing the drinking, the band or the audience, or if it mattered. Since the band was kind of a haphazard thing they never had the same members twice in a row. Band members would drift in and out as their schedules permitted. This always added a little flare to the music. Kind of like certain types of jazz where each number is an original.

The Hawk Band's most popular number was an original made up by someone in the band, called "WHEN THE HAWK IS ON THE STALK!" It was sung to the tune of "When the Saints Come Marching In". The words were simple, but inspiring:

"Oh, when the Hawk, is on the stalk,"
"Oh, when the Hawk is on the stalk."
"I want to be in that number,"
"When the Hawk is on the Stalk."

This is, of course, repeated over and over again until someone got tired and wondered why they were doing what they were doing anyway. The band had other numbers that were equally thrilling, but perhaps less motivating.

The band, unfortunately, never won any awards, but for a few moments, it took their minds off of home, or combat, or whatever may be troubling them and made the war a little more tolerable.

Another diversion was the AIROPS Cinema. Now every ship has movies for their crew. The Hawk was no exception. Every night after the evening meal, and at midnight, a movie was shown in the crew's mess. Movies were also shown in the officer's mess, and in the squadron ready rooms, but these movies lacked the luster of being forbidden, and were usually about ten years old. In addition, most of the AIROPS / CATCC crew couldn't get to the crew's movie until it was about half over. Necessity being the mother of invention, a scheme was devised to bring the movies to AIROPS. The AIROPS Cinema was however, a little different.

The Air Transfer Office, or ATO, was that entity that coordinated movement of certain of the ship's logistics that came in daily on the Carrier Onboard Delivery plane, or

COD. This included the ship's mail, passengers coming and going from the ship, and among other things, movies for the Admiral's staff aboard the Hawk. Now Rank Has Its Privileges, and first run movies was the privilege of the Admiral's staff. It so happened that the ATO was under the control of AIROPS. It also happened that one of the workers in ATO was good friends with the marine on the Admiral's staff whose responsibility it was to coordinate the movies. Through a few perks and favors, it wasn't long until AIROPS had gained access to the Admiral's movies, and the AIROPS Cinema began.

Each day or night as soon as possible after flight operations were completed, the show began. The AIROPS space could accommodate about thirty people comfortably, fifty if the movie was particularly a good one, dictating standing room only. In addition, a second showing was almost always in order for those who missed the first. Now this worked because the ship's flying schedule was usually noon-to-midnight, or midnight-to-noon, and the Admiral's staff worked banker's hours, with the movie being shown to them after dinner, about 7 p.m. Now some of the staff people knew about our arrangement, because they came to AIROPS to watch the movies. Their schedules coincided with the Hawk's air operations, and they would otherwise miss the movie. They were also okay guys, and kept quiet about it.

The AIROPS Cinema was totally illegal and underground, but it worked for eight of the nine months of the cruise. It would have worked longer, but our marine contact was transferred two weeks before we left for home. There was no rank distinction for the AIROPS Cinema. Anyone was welcome as long as there was room. Occasionally we would have seamen from the engineering department up for the flick. All we asked was that they keep quiet, both during the movie and about the cinema. It was an unwritten rule that the movie stopped at the hint of emergency flight operations, which occurred a few times. In

AIROPS and CATCC as air controllers, the work was at a very high stress level. A first run movie helped to reduce that stress before the crew retired for the night. Before showing the movie, we would extend our thanks to the Admiral (in absentia), for lending us the film. I'm sure he will never know how much he personally contributed to the war effort by his graciousness.

ATTITUDE CHECK!

Fighting a war has many aspects and many heroes. One of the marvels of war is the transformation of boys into men. This happens mentally, emotionally, and physically to the many young airmen supporting the war effort in their labors day in and day out at the many mundane jobs that have to be done.

Modern jet attack aircraft are a marvel of aviation development. They are faster, more maneuverable, more powerful and more efficient than their predecessors. They carry special electronic equipment allowing them to search out and destroy their targets with great accuracy. But, no matter how amazing they seem, in a wartime situation they still have to be loaded with ordnance. This ordnance is usually heavy, bulky and hard to handle. One of these pieces of destruction is the 500-pound bomb. This was probably the most common of weapons used by the attack birds on the Hawk.

Machinery and special equipment have been developed at great expense to load bombs. This machinery works well in its function, allowing just two persons to load a very heavy weapon. Unfortunately, this equipment is usually very slow.

Now we were fighting a war, and many birds had to be loaded with many bombs in a very short period of time. Attempts were made to use the special equipment, but it just couldn't do the job fast enough. Something had to be done. Thus, the emergence of the young ordnancman.

Most of these young men, kids if you will, were scrawny specimens, just out of high school. They joined the navy to see the world, then found out that they had to DO something to earn their keep. As most young men like to play with things that make a big bang, they decided to become ordnancmen. They attended schools to learn how to use the special equipment designed for the aircraft weaponry, even loaded dummy weapons for practice. Most had become proficient at loading a few bombs on a stationary, stable mock-up platform where time was not a consideration. None had functioned on the rushed, cramped, moving platform of an aircraft carrier in a wartime environment.

Now take these kids and place them in groups, five at a time, overseen by an experienced ordnanceman. This experienced ordnanceman was different. He was the same height as the kids, but was twice as wide and strong as an ox. He could singlehandedly take on all five of these kids at the same time and mop the floor with them. The kids soon found this out, and a strange kind of respect ensued.

There is a certain "CAN DO" attitude that men at war develop, and are very proud to maintain. These young ordnancemen were no different. The solution to the slow mechanical devices was to replace them with a team of these young ordnancemen, then put them in competition with other similar teams. It worked very well.

To an outside observer it was wonderful to see these young men work. They would, at the command of their experienced leader, align themselves along side a 500-pound bomb lying on a trolley built for the same. Then, again at the word of the leader, they would pick up this bulky weapon and as a team, raise it up above their heads into the shackles on the aircraft. Then they would hold it there until the leader inserted a safety pin securing the weapon. After this was complete, the leader, standing in front of the others, would call in a loud voice: "ATTITUDE CHECK?". The entire group in unison would yell in reply, "F*** YOU!" The group would then move to the next bomb and repeat the procedure.

When you consider the Hawk made seven launches per day, with up to twenty aircraft per launch, all loaded with between sixteen and thirty 500-pound bombs, This becomes a lot of weapons, and a lot of attitude checks. After a couple months of this, what started out as scrawny kids became well-developed, muscular young men. When you met one of these young men, you would step aside and let him pass, hoping in the process that you didn't annoy him. Their leader could no longer take on all five, but all five plus their leader could take on anything.

As the cruise progressed this team of a coach and five players made a significant change of direction. Someone discovered that four of these now in shape ordnancemen could lift the bomb easier than five because they had more room in which to work. The fifth guy was assigned to "build up" the next bomb, allowing the entire team to load the same number of weapons in a significantly shorter period of time. The team rotated such that each person lifted more per lift, but had fewer lifts overall. This concept soon caught on with most of the loading teams.

While the "ATTITUDE CHECK" amused us all, it served a very useful purpose. This bit of profanity united the team in a manner that can only be understood by those who have been in a similar circumstance. It's kind of like the offensive line on a football team. Individually they are virtually worthless, but united as a team they can get the job done.

The ordnancemen loading teams were perhaps the most visible of the many "team" operations onboard the carrier that made it work. Most did their jobs unnoticed and unsung, but without them the Hawk would not function. A successful mission by any one aircraft was in reality the culmination of the efforts of all 5500 men onboard the ship. In that sense the entire aircraft carrier acted as a team. Even so, there were times when each crewmember felt as though he was acting alone. It was during these times when the "ATTITUDE CHECK" would bring us back to reality.

ALONGAPO

The normal rotation of aircraft carriers on Yankee Station was to spend thirty days operating, called a "Line period". This was followed by a one-week break usually in the Philippines, at Naval Station Subic Bay. The southern half of the naval station was the air station, called Cubi Point. When in port, the Hawk normally tied up at the pier at Cubi Point. The town closest to the naval station was Alongapo. Cubi Point offered everything a sailor needed, and many of the crew rarely went into town. While Cubi Point offered everything that was needed it did not offer everything that was wanted. Thus, most of the crew had at least gone to town, if for nothing more than to see what was there.

Alongapo was a port town. It catered to sailors who came to town with a pocket full of money, wanting to drink and to socialize, and whatever. There were some wonderful places and people there. Unfortunately, there were some scum also. This scum had taken the art of fleecing sailors to a new height.

When going into Alongapo, sailors were advised to not take any more money than they could afford to lose, not to wear watches or any other adornment or insignias on their uniforms, and never to go alone. A lone sailor was an easy mark, and almost always resulted in some type of robbery and/or harm to the sailor.

Jeepneys were the primary transportation in Alongapo. A Jeepney was an open vehicle (originally a WWII jeep) with a driver that had two rows of seats in the back. When you rode a Jeepney, you paid the driver before boarding, then just got off when the vehicle came close to your destination. Jeepneys were used by all, not just sailors. The operators were very original in decorating their Jeepney's, hoping to attract more paying customers. They were fun to ride.

A favorite trick of some of the Alongapo scum was to board a jeepney carrying sailors and sit down next to one of them. As the vehicle bounced and rocked down the road they would carefully take a razor blade and slit the rear pants pocket of the sailor they were next to, and carefully remove his wallet. When the deed was done, the culprit would simply get off at the next stop and disappear into the crowd. Usually the sailor didn't realize his wallet was missing until he tried to pay for something, a long distance from the Jeepney and his crafty assailant.

I had the dubious distinction to be assigned as Senior Shore Patrol Officer on occasion. This duty took us to the Alongapo Police station, where we had a desk, and could intervene when a United States sailor was brought in. Unless the charge was very serious, most sailors were released into our custody. Seeing how Alongapo police run their station was an education in itself. The station was led by a desk sergeant that was a big fellow. Most Philipino people are small, but not all. This guy was BIG! Along with the desk sergeant, there were several other officers around the station and others in and out as their duties dictated. There were two holding cells just off the main room of the station that measured about eight feet by twenty feet each, without furniture. Each cell had about thirty people inside, sitting, standing, crouching, or trying to lie down.

One night at the station, one of the people inside one of the holding cells was making trouble for the rest. A number of complaints were made until finally the desk sergeant decided to solve the problem. He positioned two of his officers in front of the cells, armed with sub-machine guns. He then opened the cell detaining the troublemaker and with his policeman's club swinging wildly in his right hand, walked in. The prisoners, both male and female scattered to escape the swinging club. The sergeant quickly found the annoying culprit and picked him up by the neck, with his left hand, and brought him out. Once outside, and the cell door closed, he released the gasping prisoner, giving him to another guard who took him outside to a solitary cell. This cell was more like a cage, big enough to sit in but not much more, made totally of wire. The prisoner was left there, to be bothered by the local insects for the rest of the night.

About an hour after the cell incident a young and very intoxicated woman was brought in for using drugs. This was not her first encounter, and the decision was made to book her for further prosecution. Part of the booking procedure was to take her "mug shot". Photograph they did. The barely coherent woman was taken into a back room by her two male "photographers", stripped, photographed in every position imaginable, using several rolls of polaroid film in the process. The girl was then dressed and deposited into one of the holding cells. After locking up the accused, the officers freely passed the pictures around the room. The photographers bragged on how many angle shots they were able to make and how good a model she was.

On another occasion the Mayor of Alongapo visited the police station. This was a rather unusual experience starting with three military type personnel carriers pulling up to the station and a squad of "Police" armed with sub-machine guns positioning themselves around the building. When they determined all secure, several guards from a second vehicle came into the station, again heavily armed, and positioned themselves around the room. The mayor, a woman, then strolled through the door and addressed the sergeant. They appeared to be old friends, talking and laughing for the better part of fifteen minutes. The sergeant then introduced her to the other officers in the room, to me, and as a group, to the prisoners. She then departed in the inverse order of her appearance, and all returned to normal.

One must understand that small town politics in the Philippines often depends on who can muster the most force. The Mayor of Alongapo had succeeded her husband who had been assassinated a few months earlier. The "would be's" were not successful in wiping out the Mayor's forces, thus the man's wife took over. She was under constant threat of assassination herself and had to take heavy security precautions wherever she went.

In spite of its problems, Alongapo was a quaint town and if the proper precautions were taken, good times could be had. There was also bus service to other areas that were very scenic. The Philippines, when out of the cities, was the picture of a tropical island paradise, with beautiful beaches, warm water, volcanoes, and tropical thunderstorms. The people were very friendly, and always willing to help sailors have a good time. There were many shops filled with native goods and goods from all over Asia. Restaurants with local cuisine were plentiful. Sport fishing and diving was unsurpassed. Wildlife, especially monkeys and birds were plentiful and entertaining. Wildlife in the bars and clubs was also plentiful and the Hawk's sailors partook.

THE BRIAR AND THE ROSE

NAS Cubi Point offered many things to a recreating sailor. The Navy Exchange had an excellent selection of local crafts and electronics. After the first line period, literally hundreds of stereo systems were purchased and brought aboard the Hawk. The base gymnasium was one of the best equipped I have ever seen, offering something for all. Movies were shown several times during the day. A complete hobby shop was available, as was a bowling alley, clubs and pools for officers, chiefs, and enlisted people.

I liked to hang out at the officers' pool. I have always liked water sports, sunbathing and watching the sights around the pool. The pool also sported a bar and grill to keep us cool and fed. The claim to fame of the "pool gang" was the modified water polo games, organized at the spur of the moment from whomever was there. These games had only two rules. To score, a ball had to be put into the net. The second was that you could not drown your opponent -- everything else was legal. It was an unwritten rule that if you couldn't stand the pain, then don't get into the water. It was a time for venting the frustrations of the previous thirty days line period, and vent we did. After thirty minutes of play, everyone was thoroughly exhausted, and no longer cared about what had happened before.

There were also about twenty wives and a few school teachers that frequented the pool, improving the scenery immensely This was sometimes a problem for us horny men, especially when they showed up in bikinis. When this would happen, we would play another water ball game, then maybe another, and another. When the sun went down we would adjourn to the Officer's Club for the evening's food and entertainment.

There was a small island just offshore from the base that had been converted into a resort for sailors by the NAS Cubi Point Special Services. A boat shuttled anyone who wanted to spend a day at the beach, or boating, or fishing. The island had food and drink and shade if it got too hot. This was a favored place of many of the crew.

This was also a favored place of the senior ship's officer who had met the stewardess in Hawaii. One particular day he brought a sweet young Philipino girl to the island for a day of basking in the sun. While there he rented a boat and together they motored out into the bay, to be alone. In his efforts to show his date the sights, he wandered quite a distance from the resort, far enough to be away from the safety of patrolling navy craft. To his astonishment he discovered piracy was still being practiced in this part of the world,

Three men in a small boat overtook this officer and his date, forcing them to stop. The pirate's boat was faster and they were armed. Not expecting this treatment and having little to defend themselves with, the officer and his lady soon surrendered. The pirates were only interested in their possessions, not their craft, obviously wanting to fleece the troops but not get the Navy on their case. They took everything they had, including their money, camera and clothes, leaving them with nothing more than their undies. Their task complete, the pirates sailed away into the sunset, and disappeared to who knows where. The senior officer motored back to the resort, then returned to the ship with his lady friend, again, clad only in their boxer shorts.

Coming aboard the Hawk was always a public event and this was no exception. There were working parties on the pier, liberty parties waiting for transportation, and a few sailors just standing around waiting for something to happen. Getting aboard in nothing but your skivvies without being noticed especially as a senior officer, was just not possible. In addition, this senior officer was one that was well known by the crew. No one would dare say anything to the officer, but boy how those tongues did wag behind his back. Now add this experience to the already infamous officer's Hawaiian reputation, and you can understand why he became known as the "Briar", and the incident was subsequently referred to as the "Briar and the Rose", Once back to the ship, the "Briar" managed to suitably clothe his "Rose", and transported her to her home. It never really became known if the pirates were friends or even family of the "Rose" (which was a distinct possibility), or if she was also an innocent victim. It really didn't matter. After the embarrassment of this incident the "Briar" either changed his ways or became much craftier in his approach to his escapades and never got caught again.

After this incident the crew began openly referring to this officer as the "Briar", sometimes in his presence. As time went on the "Briar" became quite famous, having become the object of much speculation. After the tongue-waggers exploited all the facts they had, they added their own versions of fantasy embellishing the "Briar's" misdeeds, raising him to the highest level of debauchery. To my knowledge the senior officer behind all this never realized he was the "Briar"! Or possibly he knew all along and enjoyed the infamy.

LOOK MOM, I LAID AN EGG!

The A5 Vigilante is a big airplane that never worked well for what it was designed to do. It was designed with a hollow fuselage opening in the rear, that would be used for a bomb-bay to carry a nuclear weapon. The intent was that the aircraft would come in at a very low altitude underneath the enemy's radar at high speed. At a predetermined point the pilot would pull UP so as to arrive over its target heading straight up into the air. At this point the pilot would eject its bomb out the back of the fuselage, continue through the first half of a loop, then roll over and get the hell out before the weapon exploded. Upon release, the weapon would continue its upward travel until it ran out of momentum, then fall back down onto the target and explode. This supposedly would allow the delivery aircraft to get far enough away to escape the effects of the blast. A nice concept, but it just didn't work that well.

The navy in its wisdom did not want to admit a goof-up, so they replaced the bomb with a big fuel tank and installed a camera, making it a photo reconnaissance plane. This worked okay, because it was fast and had excellent low altitude navigation capability. It was a difficult aircraft to land aboard the carrier because of its size. It was also a gas hog being only slightly more efficient than the Phantoms. It was laden with electronics that were not as reliable as their designers had hoped, thus they were not operable much of the time. They become known as the "HANGAR QUEENS" of the ship.

One fine day everything worked right and the A5 Vigilante was scheduled to fly a photo mission. All looked well as it taxied onto the starboard BOW CAT. The plane was hooked up to the CAT, powered up, burners on, and bang, shot off flawlessly into the blue. All, that is, except the large fuel tank from within the bowels of the Vigilante fuselage. When the catapult pulled the Vigilante forward, the tank just simply didn't go anywhere, falling out the rear of the plane. For one brief moment the tank just sat there on the flight deck.

Human recollection of time is difficult when describing that "one brief moment", It wasn't a very long time until the large fuel tank containing perhaps 500 gallons of jet fuel exploded in a massive fireball. The ship's TV recorded the entire event, first the launch, the tank sitting there, then the explosion. Next came one of the most beautiful scenes ever witnessed from the annals of fire control history. About twenty men running in unison, emerged from a cloud of thick black smoke carrying a large hose used to deposit foam on a fire. It didn't seem that many men could react that fast together, but they did. The many hours of training for this moment paid off. A few seconds later they were applying foam to the fire.

The scene was particularly beautiful because there were ten attack planes, fully loaded with bombs, parked along the port side of the bow, and about fifty feet from the burning fuel tank. From the size of the fire we really did expect these planes to catch fire and their bombs to "cook off". Had that happened the bombs would be exploding right on top of us. The AIROPS space was just two levels below the flight deck on the port side of the ship.

The fire party excelled at their job. Within 30 seconds the fire was totally extinguished. The only damage sustained was to the Vigilante fuel tank, nothing else. One minute later we were continuing the launch on the same CAT. The Vigilante that everyone had forgotten about continued on its mission. Another aircraft checked him out and found no damage, just lighter by 5000 pounds of fuel and tank. We gave him a drink from the tanker just in case. The burned fuel tank was pushed aside to be inspected by experts to determine why it had come loose in the first place.

So close, yet so far! As is the case in many aircraft carrier emergency maneuvers, one doesn't realize how close to disaster they sometimes come. There were over 100 bombs on the attack planes overhead. That's over 25 tons of bombs, more than enough to blow off the front half of the ship! We don't know if it was just blind luck, fate or a blessing from above. We didn't care. We were just glad it came in our favor.

OPERATION KHAKI PANTS

There comes a time after working a position for a long time that certain liberties are taken to expedite the operation. I was always looking for ways to improve what was being done, and was not above trying a new trick now and then. An aircraft carrier has numerous radios. AIROPS had a number of these radios assigned to us for air control purposes. For the most part these radios were multi channel Ultra High Frequency (UHF) with "line of sight" transmission, limiting their range to 100 to 150 miles, depending upon the receiving aircraft's altitude. Another radio used by AIROPS was the Raspberry circuit. This was actually a "frequency" that was always set up on a remote radio for AIROPS use. This circuit differed from the others in that it was a low frequency, long-range radio used for aircraft control, primarily for aircraft departures and arrivals from distant bases. This frequency was for unclassified information and unlike the UHF frequencies, was probably monitored by our enemies, as well as our friends. So, particular care was taken as to what was said so as not to reveal anything of importance to the unfriendly.

It so happened that a Navy Captain serving somewhere in the Washington D.C. area, received emergency orders to the Admiral's staff serving aboard the Hawk. His orders required that he depart immediately, and report ASAP. Due to his hasty departure, there was not time for him to procure summer uniforms. It was winter in Washington D.C., also on Yankee station, but winter on Y.S. meant it only got up to 95 degrees with 90% humidity, still hot when you are wearing dress blues.

The good captain had to commandeer rides so as to reach the Hawk post haste. His travels took him to a sister ship, also on Yankee Station, where he thought he had a few hours to kill. Thus, he visited their uniform shop. He ordered several pair of khaki pants, but they didn't quite fit, so the ship's tailor set out to make the alterations. A few minutes later a flight from our sister ship to the Hawk became available, and the good Captain took it, without the much-needed khaki pants.

Soon after the good captain arrived, still attired in dress blues, he informed us of his predicament and asked if we could have his pants sent over on the next available flight. Now, I had occasion to oversee a lot of operations, but never the retrieval of khaki pants. So what the heck, we took on the job.

Not long after accepting this awesome responsibility it became known to me that the land-based COD aircraft that daily brought the mail and other important things had just recovered aboard our sister ship. It also became known that the same COD aircraft would be departing on their next launch with the Hawk as its destination. This was an unscheduled stop, and a perfect time to make the khaki pants transfer. A quick check of departure times revealed that the COD was about to leave and we needed to notify the sister ship's ATO immediately, to get the Khaki pants on the departing plane. A simple message was derived to tell all that needed to know what the plan would be. This message was sent out over the unclassified Raspberry frequency:

"Operation Khaki Pants commence 1530 local."

My counterpart on the sister ship knew exactly what to do. He directed his ATO to put the khaki pants aboard the COD that was to recover aboard the Hawk at 1530 hours.

The COD with the khaki pants arrived for the 1530 recovery, just as planned. The plane made a normal TRAP, dropped off its cargo and launched again continuing on its mission. Our ATO personally retrieved the khaki pants and took them to the newly arrived captain who was most appreciative to receive them. Everybody was happy. We all went about our business and forgot about the khaki pants.

About three weeks later a young officer from the Office of Naval Intelligence (ONI) arrived aboard the Hawk on the COD aircraft. This also was a common occurrence, as ONI always had a running dialog with the ship's communications people. What seemed different was the young ONI agent began asking questions of people from CIC and AIROPS, not communications. What was also interesting was the character of this ONI agent. He was hard boiled, so serious that those questioned felt intimidated from the start, seemingly not even capable of having a sense of humor. Strange!

The second day after the ONI agent came aboard was my turn. He arrived during a recovery and began asking me questions. I asked him to take a seat and make himself comfortable, and that after the recovery I would talk to him. This didn't sit well as ONI agents are used to having things done on their terms. About 15 minutes later we trapped the last bird, I sent the tanker up to the BARCAP, then sat back and asked the young officer what I could do for him.

"Your ship has violated the security regulations governing the use of unclassified radio circuits, specifically the use of the . . . air control circuit, called the . . . Raspberry circuit."

I asked this somber gent, who was very quick to accuse, how so, in that I was the only one who would have authorized any Raspberry transmissions, the only one who was on watch, and that certainly I would have heard any transmissions made since the transceiver was about three feet from my head.

He commenced to tell me, "On the date specified, you sir made the transmission: 'Operation Khaki Pants commence 1530 local.'"

He went on to say that the transmission of starting times for any operations was a violation of navy regulations, and that this was a very serious matter.

I don't suppose my laughter, or that of my assistants helped my situation. It certainly didn't impress the ONI agent. When I regained my composure, I made an attempt to explain operation Khaki Pants. I expected him to find the whole matter rather amusing, but, HE DIDN'T BELIEVE ME! Instead I got the "likely story" routine, and he began to explain how serious this really was and how my making a joke of it was not amusing, nor would it improve my position with higher authorities.

Okay, enough sourpuss. I cut the ONI agent off mid sentence, then laid on some of my own authority. I told the grouch that HE would have to find out about what operation Khaki Pants was, since he didn't believe me, and that if he could prove there was such a thing that I would go willingly. I also told him to layoff my helpers, and that any interrogation of them would be when I could let them have the time.

At that, the ONI agent closed his notebook, stood up and said curtly, "I will talk to you later!", then departed AIROPS.

The fool spent the next week questioning anyone who would talk to him about operation Khaki Pants. Of course, no one ever heard of it except my people, who gave him the same story I had. Finally, the agent confronted the good Captain who was the owner of the pants, again frustrated because the Captain only supported my story. He finally left, but I heard later he had gone to the AIROPS and ATO people from our sister ship, questioning, only to be frustrated with their answers. I assume he gave up the search because we never heard anything more of it, except for a general letter, criticizing how we used the Raspberry circuit with laxness and in a non-professional manner. We trashed the letter and forgot about the whole incident, I was however, glad I would not be spending some of my future in Leavenworth over several pairs of khaki pants.

I always wondered about the "Big Brother" tactics of ONI. It sure seemed to me they could better spend their time on real problems, and not chasing ghosts.

YUMMY, YUMMY, YUMMY!

Being away from home for months at a time was never an easy thing to do. Nothing can counter the loneliness and longing for home each man felt. The military doesn't even try -- they just make other things a little better so that everyone can cope. The time we spent working on Yankee station went by fast because we didn't have much time to think of home. Oddly enough, it was the time spent on "rest and recreation" that was the hardest. Next in line was the time transiting from one point to another.

The clubs at Cubi Point each had various recreational activities to offer. I am most familiar with the Officer's Club. The Q'club offered the usual things, such as cheap drinks and good food. The food on the Hawk was usually pretty good, it was the choice that left something to be desired. You could at least order whatever sounded good at the O'club. Most of us ate there because it was a change of scene, and, there was entertainment.

When a bunch of pilots get together who have just spent the last thirty days avoiding getting their butts shot up, and working very hard, it's not hard to get a party going. There didn't have to be a reason, or perhaps having survived was the reason, whatever. Work that had to be done at the ship was usually complete by noon. Slowly thereafter, the ship and air wing people would arrive and begin their day and evening's serious drinking and partying. As at all similar places where the spirits flowed, Cubi O'club had its variety of drinkers. Some tried to drink the bar dry in the shortest period of time possible. These usually went to sleep early and missed most of the fun. Others would buy one drink and have it the entire evening, sometimes not even drinking any of it, but had it just for the appearance. Most had enough to unwind, and by 7 p.m. the place was jumping.

When pilots get together and start drinking the subject of conversation usually ends up about flying. Pilots are a lot like fishermen. The risks and close calls become more and more serious and spectacular as the night, and the drinking, goes on. On occasion at Cubi, these devoted members of the liars club would really get wound up and suddenly develop the urge to act out their experiences.

The main bar and dining room was set at two levels, the bar being on one side about six steps above the dance floor and dining area. Along the bar were a number of loose stools, without casters. But, across from the bar were a few tables, each with chairs that easily rolled across the hard carpeting. As the party reached its peak of frenzy, the pilots would decide to give their compatriots a "CAT SHOT", I'm not sure how it was determined who was to get the shot. It may have been the biggest liar, or the worst. It may have been both, but whomever was chosen was placed in one of the easily rolling chairs. He was then taken all the way up the length of the bar, while the deck was being cleared, then with a burst of speed, pushed the full length of the bar, accelerating all the way, then catapulted into the air off the stairs and onto the dance floor. The superior ability of the pilot was determined, if he could maintain his chair in such a position that he landed upright and rolled to a stop. If the pilot couldn't control the chair and "crashed", he was a klutz.

These escapades always brought an uproar of approval from the crowd, The pilot, whether superior or a klutz, became a hero, thus it was a desirable thing to be the recipient of a "CAT SHOT". What was not so desirable was the bill for broken chairs that inevitably followed. Uncle Sam was not willing to bankroll this type of behavior, and the guilty parties had to fork over the cash.

CAT SHOTS were not always a nightly occurrence. What always came nightly was the band. The band was Philipino, and very responsive to the desires of the crowd. If one had a request, the band was game, playing the number to the best of their ability. Their "best" was always excellent, and we enjoyed their performances. What we enjoyed even more was their lead singer!

It's probably not too hard to excite a group of lonely men, the most saintly of whom were well down the road to lechery. But this woman was without a doubt the best-looking bundle of female flesh in all the Philippines, perhaps the world! Not only did she have the equipment, she had class. Enough class to stay just a little aloof from the crowd of groveling males in front of her. When she wasn't singing she sat in a chair behind the band and in such a position that she was protected from what she must have thought were packs of wild dogs in men's bodies. She never wore dresses that were risqué, but they did reveal the shape of her gorgeous body, which resulted in exciting the masses even more.

The crowning glory of this lady's performance was when she responded to sing the crowd's most wanted song. Everyone knew the prelude music that led to this song, so when the band began to play a hush fell over the crowd and all attention was focused on the singer.

"Yummy, yummy, yummy, I've got love in my tummy . . . " The words came out like chimes from a bell, and the crowd exploded with ecstasy. All the men in the building stood up and cheered. Clapping in time with the music, and all probably with the same thoughts. This would last for a full five minutes and when she finished everyone was exhausted. I don't know if the song had any other words. It didn't matter. What was important was that this classy woman had sung to each of us individually, or so it seemed, in her most sensuous way. She had the entire room worshiping her at her feet. She and the band would always take a break after this song, probably out of self-preservation. We also needed the break to recuperate.

It was always interesting to observe the reaction of the few women present when all the men exploded into this sensual frenzy. There was a strange sense of acceptance of the men's behavior, but almost always with great reserve. I suppose these women couldn't help but become somewhat excited because of the level of ecstasy achieved by the men, or was it a reserve coming from self-preservation? After all, they were outnumbered about 30 to one. Somewhat like being in the middle of a shark feeding frenzy.

I heard "Yummy, Yummy, Yummy" only one time back in the states. The lyrics were probably "X" rated, and totally against FCC regulations. I don't know and I really don't care, for all I heard was the first line, and my mind was back in the Cubi Q'club.

THE HAWK AIRLINES

There were a number of pilots assigned to the ship's company that had jobs that did not involve flying. Often times they had jobs like mine that kept them "tied to a desk" during flight operations. The navy requires all of its pilots to maintain proficiency by flying a minimum number of hours each month, and each year. It was usually difficult to schedule flight time while at sea, therefore we made the most of it when we were in port.

While sailing back to the Philippines after a line period on Yankee Station, AIROPS would contact each pilot and assign them to the in-port flight schedule. Collectively, the time each pilot wanted to fly usually came out about the same as the time available, so this was rarely a problem. What was more of a problem was what to do while flying. Although all of us had done it, boring holes in the sky for no reason was the least desirable thing to do with the time, and there is only a certain number of things to see from the air in that part of the world. Thus evolved the HAWK AIRLINES. The ship's only assigned aircraft, a C1, was normally launched during the last day of flight operations, and flew from Yankee station to Cubi Point. When the ship arrived the C1 was ready for whatever had been scheduled,

People are always moving. We are a mobile lot, never wanting to stay put in anyone place for very long. The primary mode of transportation around that part of the Philippines was the bus. The buses were of the "school bus" variety, with windows that opened, allowing dust, grime and insects to blow in, joining the dust, grime and insects already inhabiting the vehicle. Roads were never smooth, and it was always HOT. Clark Air Force base took about two hours, Manila four. The prime mountain resort of Bagio took all day with several "transfers", Thus, when the word was out that certain authorized personnel could fly, the HAWK AIRLINES had plenty of takers.

We did not discriminate as to who boarded the aircraft. The base Air Transportation Office took care of that. All we had to do was inform the base ATO how many seats we had available and where we were going. Once aboard, one of the pilots would make the usual briefing we all receive when flying an airliner and make sure everyone was strapped in. We would then make a little round robin flight, first to Clark AFB, then Bagio, then Manila International airport, followed by a little sightseeing trip around the island of Corregador of World War II fame, then back to Cubi Point, all the while dropping off and picking up passengers. Although it was never officially directed or requested that this be done, all the carrier's crews did it and a problem was solved. The planes would have flown anyway, so it didn't cost Uncle Sam anything extra, and the pilots involved were glad to be of service.

It was sometimes unnerving however, like the time my roommate and I picked up a load of school teachers returning to Clark AFB, who had come to Cubi Point to party for the weekend. I was the one making sure everyone was properly strapped in. It so happened one of these young ladies couldn't get her seat belt fastened and asked me for assistance. I obliged her only to discover as I leaned over to fasten the belt that she was wearing a very short skirt and little else. I was naive enough to be embarrassed, realizing later that I had been "set up" by my roommate, when each of the girls came up and gave him and me an unsolicited goodbye kiss before deplaning.

We would on occasion stop at Bagio or Manila and go into town for a few hours. Bagio was particularly beautiful in its mountain setting, and it was COOL! It was okay to have lunch or shop a bit, but I didn't like leaving the plane unattended for very long. The airstrip was just that: A short landing strip on top of a hill with no overruns and a very small, unattended parking area.

One of the highlights of running the HAWK AIRLINE was flying over the many small beaches and villages along the coast. There were many beaches, from 500 to 2000 feet long with several "huts" just off the beach. The scene was out of a dream of what it must be in the South Pacific, absolutely beautiful. Most of these small beaches and villages could only be accessed by water, as they were not connected by roads to civilization.

Another point of interest was the extent of fisheries in Manila Bay. Most of the bay was not very deep. These shallow areas were dotted with fish traps, held in place by poles driven into the bottom. Occasionally a fisherman had built his house on stilts near one of these traps, always having a boat or two tied up to the decking. It was very scenic. We had a good time!

DONALD L HOWE

ALONE IN THE DARK!

Flying over water in an uninhabited sea on a dark night sometimes redefines the interpretation of DARK. Conditions sometimes exist that makes this type of night operation akin to flying in a huge inkwell. Any source of light seems to be immediately swallowed up in the blackness. One can become very aware of being alone in the dark.

The A7 was the only plane aboard the Hawk that had only one pilot and no other crewmembers. The A7 pilot had to accomplish all that had to be done, such as communications, fuel planning, setting up and dropping his bombs, navigation, etc. This had to be done while flying the plane, and became most critical during the approach phase of the flight when the aircraft was descending from altitude back to the ship. This was especially true when flying in the "INKWELL".

Instrument flying is accomplished by thousands of pilots everyday, and the procedures are not difficult. There are certain dangers, however, that each pilot must recognize and take measures to avoid. It is very easy to become disorientated while flying instruments because there is no reference to the ground, or the horizon. An instrument-equipped aircraft has an "Attitude Gyro" or some other instrument that shows the pilot an artificial horizon, allowing him to maintain the proper flight attitude without actually seeing the ground. This instrument is very necessary while flying in INKWELL conditions. Another danger is "VERTIGO". This is a condition caused within the inner ear, brought about by sudden turns. The sensation is that of turning or continuing to turn when you actually are not. When experiencing vertigo, a pilot MUST rely on his instruments, even though his senses tell him they are wrong.

When an aircraft makes an instrument approach to a carrier, it begins from a "fixed" location on the ship's TACAN. TACAN is a radio navigation system that tells the pilot bearing and distance information. This allows the pilot to follow a prescribed course with relation to the ship, through the clouds or darkness, ultimately leading to visual contact with the ship. The pilot then makes a "manual" or conventional landing, or an "automatic" landing with the ACLS. Sometimes the course the aircraft must follow requires a turn such that the aircraft flies an arc around the ship, until it can make its final lineup. "FINAL" is that segment of the approach where the aircraft is heading straight down the runway of the ship, within a mile or two of touchdown. "SHORT FINAL" is where the aircraft is within about one fourth mile, ready to touchdown. A "LONG FINAL" or "LONG STRAIGHT IN" approach means the aircraft is aligned with the ship's runway while still some distance out, making an "Airliner type of approach. Most instrument approaches utilized a LONG FINAL to allow the pilot a little more time to prepare for the TRAP, and shake out any vertigo that may have been induced by turns performed.

The Hawk was recovering aircraft one night where INKWELL conditions existed. The weather at the ship was not bad, but there was a layer of clouds from 2000 feet up to 10,000 feet. The recovery was progressing without any unusual events until the A7'S were approaching. The approach controller gave instructions to one A7 to make a right turn to the final approach radial, of about 40 degrees. The A7 at that point was passing through 7000 feet, descending to 3000 feet. The pilot acknowledged the turn and altitude instructions on the approach control frequency. The approach controller observed the plane begin its turn on the radar, then lost contact.

The point of lost contact was about fifteen miles behind the ship, in about a seven o'clock position. The HOOKIE and the plane guard destroyer were both detached to begin a search and rescue operation. The HOOKIE was on station a few minutes later, but could find no sign of the downed aircraft, or its pilot. The destroyer arrived about one half hour later and conducted an extensive search for the next few days. No evidence of the plane or ill-fated pilot was ever found.

It was surmised by the Accident Investigation Board that the pilot had either developed a bad case of vertigo, or had been the victim of a fatal heart attack. A third possibility of carbon monoxide poisoning was also discussed. Having never found the pilot's body left the matter open for doubt as to the cause.

It is never easy for a controller to lose one of his aircraft. In this incident the controller was not at fault. The procedures and communications used were found to be standard, and no act of the controller contributed to the incident. There was no indication from the approach control frequency recordings that the pilot was under any kind of distress, or experiencing any danger. All this doesn't help a conscientious controller, who no matter what conditions causes an accident, blames himself. It is not uncommon for controllers to have a nervous breakdown when this occurs, or to quit the business altogether. We did not want this to happen, and put the individual back to work on the radar, with reassurance from his fellow controllers, and a little closer supervision for a time. He came through the incident fine.

This is the only aircraft lost while under control of AIROPS / CATCC, during two nine-month combat cruises. We had other losses for various reasons, such as hostile operations, mechanical problems, even pilot errors, etc. but never while under our control. This was also the only incident that occurred where the reason was not positively determined. We, like every other carrier, tried very hard not to lose anyone. We were proud of our record. We were also VERY LUCKY!

WHO WORKS FOR WHOM?

There is and always will be a certain professional pride between different branches of the armed forces. This pride only becomes stronger during wartime, sometimes to the point where judgment is impaired, and the ridiculous ensues.

The Hawk had a requirement to keep a certain amount of fuel available in the air for returning birds that may be a little short or have trouble getting aboard. We also gave a certain amount away to the "BARCAP" or BARRIER COMBAT AIR PATROL. The BARCAP was usually two F4 Phantoms positioned in the northern Tonkin Gulf, under the control of a destroyer, used to defend the fleet against a surprise airborne attack. It could have been more F4's if the threat dictated, but two usually could do the job. If an aircraft came out of North Vietnam into the Tonkin Gulf, the F4's would intercept and destroy. I suppose that the U.S. at some point had declared the Gulf as a war zone, therefore when an enemy plane became "feet wet" or over the water, he was fair game. We usually gave the F4's about 5000 pounds of fuel, giving them a "combat package" of fuel in case of intercept.

One day when the weather was particularly crappy, the tanker getting ready to launch went down mechanically and could not go. The tanker skipper and I discussed what we could do. Double cycling the tanker that was airborne (to have it cover two recoveries without landing) would not solve the problem in that we would have to give some fuel away to the recovering birds due to the weather. Double cycling reduced the available fuel by the amount the tanker needed to stay airborne the extra time, usually leaving 5000 to 7000 pounds giveaway. Giving 5000 pounds to the BARCAP left little to nothing for the recovering birds.

Now the Air Force had a mission to provide fuel to returning aircraft operating out of Danang. They would normally have a KC135 on station in a holding pattern, just off of Danang, which was about 120 miles away from us. The tanker skipper and I decided to send our tanker over to the Air force tanker, pick up about 20,000 pounds of fuel, then come back and service our needs on a double cycle. We checked the departure control radar, and sure enough, the KC135 was there. Now, the KC135 carries more giveaway fuel than our entire launch used. There wasn't a question of whether the fuel was available -- it was there for anyone needing it, friendly that is.

I called our ship's CIC or the Combat Information Center who had primary control of our aircraft in the area of the KC135 and informed them of our plan, asking if they would take control of our tanker and direct him to the Air Force tanker.

A long pause ensued.

I was informed by the CIC watch officer that we couldn't do that. I asked why not, and was told, "because the staff didn't approve it."

I informed the CIC watch officer that I didn't ask the staff, nor did I need their permission. I then repeated my request to send our tanker to the KC135.

I was again notified that they wouldn't do it, and that they were going to have a sister carrier (that was in its sleep cycle) launch a tanker to cover the BARCAP since we couldn't. When I asked why we couldn't just get the fuel as we planned, I was told we couldn't because the KC135 was from the Air Force.

The conversation had progressed so far into the ridiculous that I couldn't resist. I answered:

"I didn't know the Air Force was fighting for the North Vietnamese? I always thought we were on the same side!"

At that the CIC watch officer said he didn't want to have any part of what we were doing, and he wouldn't take any responsibility for it. I agreed, and accepted all responsibility, I then informed my own departure controller to send the tanker to the KC135 and take on about 20,000 pounds of fuel.

Our tanker flew over to the KC135, took on 24,000 pounds of fuel (The Air Force tanker would have willingly given them twice that amount). Our tanker then returned, covered our recovery, serviced the BARCAP, and came back to the Hawk for the next recovery with 12,000 pounds giveaway fuel. It worked like clockwork.

I'll never cease to be amazed at how some people can be promoted and assigned to responsible positions who are incapable of making decisions. The attitude seemed to be that we were being graded on how well we observed military protocol, not on how well we fought the damned war!

A THING OF BEAUTY

Nothing is quite as exciting as when everything you have practiced, coordinated or executed comes together as planned. This is especially sweet when it happens during a "real time" emergency situation.

We made a routine launch while on Yankee station. It was about 4 pm and the weather was good. Not long after one particular A7 launched we received a distress call on departure control frequency. This particular A7 was flown by the skipper of the squadron, a very experienced pilot generally and in that type of aircraft. He was experiencing difficulty with his engine and wanted to return to the ship. The departure controller gave him a vector back to the ship, to join the visual recovery in progress.

I don't know why but my instincts said to send the rescue helicopter. I called the AIRBOSS who had control, and requested he vector the HOOKIE out 170 degrees at about 40 miles. The AIRBOSS had also heard the distress call and agreed with my request. The HOOKIE was sent "BUSTER", which meant to proceed at max speed, on the vector given.

No sooner had the helicopter departed when the pilot in distress notified us that his engine had failed and he was going to "punch out". He then ejected from the disabled craft, parachuting to the water. The plane, of course, crashed into the water well clear of anything on the surface.

The HOOKIE arrived in the area and immediately gained visual contact with the pilot who was still descending in his parachute. The rescue bird had to stand off until the pilot hit the water and got out of and clear of his parachute. (Making a rescue with the pilot still in the parachute is very dangerous in that the pilot can get tangled up in the shroud line of the parachute and be dragged under the water by the action of the helicopter's prop wash.) Once the pilot was clear, the HOOKIE went in, picked him up and returned to the ship.

The whole operation took about fifteen minutes, which is about the time it would take for the aircraft to travel the distances involved. The pilot was brought back to the ship, checked out by the medical staff and returned to duty. He could have flown the next launch! There were fewer than 6 transmissions made on the radio and the intercom to report the problem, execute the rescue and get the pilot back onto the ship. Everything was almost automatic. It was gratifying to see where training had paid off. It truly was "A THING OF BEAUTY".

UNREPS

Wars can only be fought over a sustained period of time when adequate logistical support is provided. While the Hawk was a big ship, it was also a working ship, supporting more that one hundred aircraft sorties each day of flight operations. This took fuel for the planes and the ship, ammunition and ordnance, spare parts, food and other supplies. A carrier cannot carry enough of these items to operate continuously for extended periods. To solve this problem the navy has developed "UNDERWAY REPLENISHMENT" or "UNREPS".

If wars were fought just off your own coast replenishment would not be a problem. Aircraft carriers were developed to extend a country's power so a war would not have to be fought close to home. It is much safer to bring the replenishment to the ship. Underway Replenishment has been developed into an ART that probably can be appreciated only when it has been witnessed. I'm sure the thought of bringing two massive ships together to within about 100 feet, gives both Captains nightmares.

The Hawk would receive UNREPS of some sort at least every other day while operating on Yankee Station. Some days it would be fuel from a tanker ship. Some days bombs and other ammunition. Some days provisions, and some days all of the above. The supply ship would stand off waiting for flight operations to cease. Once flight ops were complete, both ships would take up a course so as to rendezvous, then take up a common course, paralleling each other at 100 to 150 feet apart. Lines were then shot across, followed by ropes or cables, then hoses. The cables and hoses were secured with enough tension to keep them out of the water, then the transfer of supplies began.

Liquid transfer was probably the simplest. Transfer of other goods was accomplished by placing pallets of goods on a huge nylon cargo net that was picked up by each corner, hooked to a trolley, raised to clear the deck, then drawn from the supply ship to the Hawk. A third method of transfer was to use helicopters.

A CH46 was the primary helicopter used. It was assigned to the supply ship, and transferring supplies was their entire mission. The helo transfer would also use the supply net concept, but was much faster than using a cable trolley arrangement. The helo would simply hover over its intended load while the deck crew hooked up the net. It would then add power and begin a climb. When the cargo was clear of the supply ship, a gentle turn toward the carrier was begun. The helo would align itself with the carrier's flight deck, then descend until the cargo was safely resting aboard the ship. The helo pilot then activated a quick disconnect releasing the cargo. Once clear, the helo motored back to the supply ship and started the procedure over again. During an UNREP this was repeated hundreds of times.

An UNREP lasted from two to four hours, depending on the weather and how much the supply ship had to give the Hawk. Keeping the two massive craft on an exactly parallel course with just the right tension on the lines between the two was a minor miracle in itself. Both ships produced a "BOW WAVE" motion of the water that had to be constantly counteracted. Consider both ships forcing water to the sides, and this water being trapped between the ships, having no place to go. A tremendous pressure begins to build, trying to push the vessels apart. Now add the motion of the sea, acting on each ship differently, and a very complicated control problem develops.

Perhaps a greater problem was putting it all together in the first place. When one figures that the material has to procured, shipped to some point of departure, loaded aboard the supply ship, then transported across thousands of miles of ocean so as to arrive at exactly the right time and place. IT IS MIND BOGGLING! This, I'm sure, took months of planning, and a lot of educated guesses. Whoever was responsible for it did their job very well. I can't remember a single time or incident where we were wanting for supplies.

Once the UNREP was complete, the lines and hoses were disconnected and reeled in, so as not to get fouled up in either ship's screws, then the ships parted company. The Hawk would usually pull away from the slower supply ships, before a turn was initiated. The Hawk would then head back to set up for the next day's (or night's) flight operations. The supply ship would head back to port to reload. It was not uncommon to see the same supply ship two or three times during a thirty-day line period.

To those actively engaged in the UNREP it was a lot of work in a short period of time. To those of us who had the luxury of just observing, the UNREP was a thing of beauty. The entire flight deck and the hangar deck next to the huge elevators bustled with activity, as did many of the areas throughout the interior of the ship where supplies were being stored. Seeing this mass of coordinated activity was almost as impressive as watching our normal flight operations.

A SIDEWINDER FOR BREAKFAST

Fighting a war with an aircraft carrier obviously requires loading planes up with bombs, launching them on missions where these bombs are dropped, and the planes returning home clean. If for some reason something goes wrong and a plane cannot drop its bombs, another part of its equipment allows the bombs to be jettisoned somewhere in a safe area. This doesn't hold true for the carrier's fighters who in a war like Vietnam, didn't often tangle with the enemy. The Hawk's fighters were F4S, and their primary weaponry was the Sidewinder, a heat-seeking missile.

The F4s ALWAYS carried Sidewinders, both launching and recovering aboard the ship. That was the normal procedure and from experience, found to be safe. The Sidewinder missile was designed to home in and fly up the tailpipe of an enemy aircraft, exploding in very close proximity of the target. Thus, the missile did not require a large explosive charge to do its job. The missile itself could do considerable damage to an aircraft, but was not much of a threat to a ship.

Recovery aboard a carrier is a very exciting experience. When brought to the point of landing, the aircraft touches down and almost immediately catches a wire with its arresting hook. This wire or arresting cable is attached at each end to energy absorbing devices that rapidly cause the aircraft to decelerate, coming to a stop in a very short distance. For the pilots, this arrested landing was always interesting because as the aircraft stopped, their bodies tried to continue forward, being restrained by their seatbelts.

These same forces of deceleration act upon everything in the aircraft. Everything had to be restrained. Thus, coming aboard with a 500-pound bomb or two really wasn't a good idea, but Sidewinders were okay. Or so we thought.

Before a pilot boards his aircraft, he conducts a preflight check. One of the items checked is the security of the weaponry, including missiles. If the missiles are not used they are checked again after landing. Sidewinders were not usually downloaded, but were checked again by an ordnancman, and the next pilot to launch. Theoretically, many eyes inspect the aircraft and the weapons before they fly.

One balmy afternoon during a visual recovery, an F4 approached for landing. His lineup was slightly off, but not enough for the LSO to wave him off, so he continued in for a landing. His touchdown was normal, and the plane TRAPPED, but one of his Sidewinder missiles didn't. The sidewinder came off, hurtling onto the deck, heading toward the bow of the ship. Due to the lineup of the aircraft, the missile didn't head off the angle deck into the water, but instead, ran up the port side of the bow, then off the ship directly in front of it.

The captain observed the missile coming off the landing aircraft. Not knowing what kind of weapon it was, he ordered an immediate hard turn to the port. This may sound like the captain was trying to hit the missile, but when you turn a ship, the stern actually makes the turn and this maneuver opened the distance between the ship and the missile. The missile didn't explode and no damage resulted.

The ship resumed its original heading and completed the recovery.

What was really amazing about this entire incident is not that the ship escaped damage. A Sidewinder probably wouldn't even make a dent in the hull if it blew up at point blank range. What was of greater note was the line of aircraft positioned for the next launch along the port side of the bow, fully loaded with bombs. The Sidewinder missile, while making its trip up the length of the ship, went completely underneath these aircraft, without striking any of them.

NATURE'S LITTLE THINGS

When flight operations were complete, the flight deck crew re-spotted the aircraft enabling maintenance crews to correct discrepancies, and opened the deck to support UNREPS, as necessary. Once this was complete, the flight deck became an enormous playing field, or observation deck as the case may be.

It was always interesting to take a position somewhere along the bow and watch the animals of the sea. Perhaps I have a simple mind, but these creatures were always intriguing, and one never knew what would show up. There was always several species of birds, almost always some flying fish, most of the time some sea snakes, and occasionally dolphins.

Flying fish seem to inhabit the entire ocean. They could be seen easily from the flight deck of the Hawk, in such a vantage point as to see them before they actually became airborne. They ranged in size from very small to very large, as flying fish go. What was most amazing was how far they could travel while airborne. Flying fish don't actually fly, in that they don't flap their fins. What happens is they accelerate under the water then leap into the air at or near the crown of a swell, then glide into the wind. They will sometimes glide to a partial landing, swim for a bit on the surface of the water then get airborne again. For lack of anything better to do, we would sometimes take bets as to how far they could travel.

Sea snakes were seen occasionally in the open ocean, but were very common in the Tonkin Gulf. There were several varieties ranging in color from a basic yellow to light green. The adults seemed to be about six feet long. All were excellent swimmers. Sea snakes are among the most venomous reptiles in the world. It was interesting that they never seemed to be doing anything except perhaps sunbathing on the surface of the water. It is said that sea snakes are not the least bit aggressive, even allowing fishermen to handle them if they happened to get hung up in their nets. We were not about to find out. They were interesting to watch, and there were many to look at.

The variety of birds in the open ocean is amazing. Many of these creatures are land based, yet are found hundreds of miles at sea. Hours could be spent counting different varieties including Seagulls, Albatross, Pelicans and Cormorants. The Albatross is probably one of the most graceful birds in flight. Its slow, easy motions just inches above a raging sea was always enjoyable to watch. There were times when I was certain the birds would crash or be swallowed up by a breaking wave, but they always managed to stay just a little ahead of or over danger.

Dolphins were occasional playmates of the ship. I was always amused by their speed. The ship could be steaming at 25 knots with dolphins playfully crossing back and forth across the bow wave. Then all of a sudden, they would shoot out in front of the ship at a speed at least twice that of ours, or so it seemed.

Sometimes when the ship was cruising at low speeds schools of fish could be seen. An occasional whale and sharks were also observed. It seemed as if they didn't mind our intrusion of their space. Sometimes they were as interested in us as we were in them. It was like they really didn't care about our silly war. Their world would be the same regardless of how humans treated each other. Sometimes I wondered if they were really smarter than we.

BANGKOK

It wasn't often I was allowed to leave the ship during flight operations, but one day I was the only co-pilot that could be made available. It was the last day the Hawk was to be on the line, with only two more launches and recoveries until the ship was due to depart for the Philippines. The flight was to take a staff officer to Nakom Phanon, in northeastern Thailand. The staff officer had business for the day of the flight and most of the next. We were to drop him off, wait for him to conclude his business, proceed back to Danang to refuel, then take the C1 on to Cubi Point. We would then meet the ship when it arrived two days later.

We launched without event, flew across the northern end of South Vietnam and Laos. The countryside was devastated, even from our 12,000 feet elevation, being full of craters made by the bombs from our planes. We would like to have taken a closer look, but they were still shooting at each other on the ground below us and the C1 was not well equipped for combat. We proceeded to Nakom Phanon, a small field belonging to the Thai Air Force, nestled in the jungle next to a small village. The staff officer we were transporting was met by his party, and we were left to fend for ourselves.

The pilot (and plane commander), who I will call Mac, went into operation to investigate the possibility of our proceeding to Bangkok. Twenty-four-hour advance notice was normally required for U.S. planes and personnel to visit Bangkok, but we had made no such request. When Mac called Bangkok via landline, he was informed that since it was Sunday, no one was there who could give us permission to proceed. Mac, having a great desire to go to Bangkok then decided that if there was no one there to tell us we could come, there was also no one there to tell us we could NOT come. So we filed a flight plan and motored off to Bangkok.

Bangkok was great! We landed at the local Thai Air Force Base. It was like going to Southern California on a warm spring day. We found a taxi that took us the twenty or so miles into town to a hotel that had been rented by the U.S. to be used by military personnel on R&R. We spent that day and night and the next morning touring the town and having a marvelous time.

Mac and I returned to our aircraft about noon. Since the previous day was Sunday, it had not been serviced or refueled. We made arrangements for refueling while we filed a flight plan back to Danang. The Thai Air Force people were not too anxious to refuel our plane because they couldn't find any authorization for our being there. Now, Mac was a great talker. Actually, this does not do him justice. Mac could lay down a line of BS so smoothly, that most were well into it before they realized they were being had. The poor Thais were not any different. His story went something like this: We were sent on an emergency mission to take a special classified message to an officer in Bangkok. The matter had come up so suddenly, that no time was available to send the necessary requests. Mac then assured them that these authorizations would be coming very soon, but that we could not wait because we had to pick up another staff officer at Nakom Phanon. Of course, after talking to them they felt the entire war effort depended upon our completing our mission, and readily gave us fuel and assistance.

We proceeded back to Nakom Phanon. When within radio range of the field we were informed that the staff officer had already departed on a flight to Danang. We changed our flight plan in the air, to make Danang our destination.

Danang was a very busy airfield. The Marines ran the field, but both Marines and Air Force planes operated from it, in support of the war effort. The Navy had a small detachment that normally serviced Navy planes that was located on the west side of the runway. The Marine side of the field, where base operations was located was on the east side of the runway. We were headed for Cubi Point, requiring we file a flight plan with base operations, so we thought we would save some time by going directly to the east side, letting the marines refuel us. This was done frequently, and we felt we were doing the right thing. It was evening at this point, and Cubi Point was 1000 miles away, about a five-hour flight.

After filing a flight plan, we loaded up a few passengers from the base ATO, and took off for Cubi Point. The flight was uneventful, and we landed at Cubi Point about midnight.

Mac and I walked into base operations and were met by a frantic operations Duty Officer. We were to refuel and return immediately to the Hawk on Yankee Station. It seems that the Hawk's orders had been changed, and it was to remain on Yankee Station for another 30-day line period. One of our sister carriers had developed a difficulty that had to be repaired, and the Hawk was extended to cover the open period. Word to this effect had been left with the Navy detachment at Danang, who we never saw, but no one thought to notify the Marines!

Now Mac and I were exhausted. We had very little sleep the night before, and had been flying the better part of both previous days. Mac told the distraught duty officer that we would NOT be going back to the ship until the next day, and that we would be back for the last recovery at noon. When asked why, Mac told the truth, "crew rest".

When the Hawk received the message, we were not returning until the next day at noon because of "crew rest" they came unglued! What had we, the crew, been doing for the past two days other than "resting"? (They were still not aware we had gone to Bangkok.) It didn't matter what the ship thought because we had gone to the Bachelor Officer's Quarters and were asleep when the return message came.

The next morning, we loaded the C1 and returned to the Hawk. We arrived for the last recovery, and were the last aircraft to TRAP. As it turned out, the ship didn't have anything in particular that had to be done. They were upset because we went to Bangkok, but not because it was the wrong thing to do, rather it was because we got to go and they didn't. I'm sure the Duty Officer in Bangkok is still waiting for our special orders to come in and is proud to know that he helped with the war effort by sending us quickly on our way.

WOULD YOU LIKE A FLOWER, MADAME?

About midway through the cruise, the Hawk was to sail into Hong Kong for a week of rest and recreation. The plan called for the ship to depart Yankee station for Subic Bay in the Philippines, remain there for three days replenishing supplies, then sail to Hong Kong. After departing Hong Kong, the Hawk would then return to Yankee station for another 30-day line operations period.

Many of the wives of ship and airwing personnel had made arrangements to visit the Philippines and Hong Kong to coincide with the visit by the Hawk, and their husbands. There were enough wives to fill a commercial airliner, and much advance planning had gone into the arrangements.

Some of us decided for various reasons that we would not have our wives visit. The reasons varied but most of us could not bear another good-by, and felt it would be better not to see our wives until the cruise was complete and we could go home to stay. As the time arrived for the wive's contingent to arrive, we were not sure we had made the right decision.

Such was the case with my assistant, who I will call Chuck. Chuck was a very likable guy, that didn't have a malicious bone in his body, He loved people, and would give you the shirt off his back if you asked for it. Chuck dearly loved his wife and his children. He talked about them all the time, especially when he received pictures from home. He would never have done anything to endanger these relationships. Chuck had one problem that was actually an asset. He had a quick wit, combined with a sharp tongue of the Don Rickles style. He never meant any harm, but always seemed to end up in trouble because of something he said. Or, at least he thought he was in trouble. Those of us who knew him knew different.

It was always a pleasure to be around Chuck. His humor kept everyone laughing, helping the time to pass quickly. It was always funny to watch him squirm when he thought he had said something he shouldn't have and was in trouble. Even his profession of vulgarity was amusing. When he suspected he was in trouble he would say: "Oh f***! I've done it again". Now this expression from most would be a turnoff, but from Chuck, it was hilarious. He would NEVER use that language in front of a female, especially his wife, who, he would claim, would "hit him with the nearest blunt instrument!" Almost everyone appreciated his humor, but apparently not all.

Chuck was somewhat distraught when we arrived in port and the wive's contingent was standing on the pier, waiting to greet their husbands. Not unusual, as those of us whose wives didn't come all felt that way. When we went ashore we did our usual thing, ending up at the Officer's Club for dinner. Chuck rarely drank more than one or two drinks a night. That night he and his friends were drinking a little more than usual. Many of the visiting wives were at the Officer's Club. Their presence only added to the gloom Chuck and his friends felt, so they decided to leave and go into Alongapo.

The group was pretty "happy" when they left for town. All seemed to go well as they arrived at one of the local clubs. Chuck stopped the group just outside the club, and proceeded to buy two handfuls of flowers from a street vendor. The group then went into the club, found a table and sat down, except for Chuck. Chuck went around the room and presented a flower to each female present. It didn't matter how old, how ugly or beautiful, or whether they were with someone else. He just made a universal presentation of this small floral gift, given with dignity and a "would you like a flower, Madame?", recognizing each girl as a human being. By the time Chuck had finished his little quest and returned to his friends at their table he found that someone had bought him a drink. He also found that as soon as he finished that drink, there was another in its place, and another and so on.

Chuck never bought a drink that whole night. The party rolled well into the early hours. Chuck was having such a good time that he did a solo dance atop the bar to one of his favorite tunes played by the band. This was followed by dancing with most, if not all, of the girls there. Whatever his antics, the entire crowd cheered him on. Chuck was in heaven!

The next day Chuck walked very slowly into AIROPS around noon. The slightest noise sent him reeling in pain. He sat down putting his head in his hands asking, "what have I done? What have I done?" We all knew what he had done. The entire ship knew what he had done. For that matter, all of Alongapo knew what he had done, perhaps all of the Philippines. It was amazing that this one individual, in a simple act of kindness, cemented international relations in a people to people act beyond anything the government could have done. The incident was talked about in town for months after. Chuck could walk on water. He was an honest to goodness hero! Chuck didn't remember anything.

About three weeks later, when we were back on Yankee station, Chuck received a letter from his wife. It was obvious that Chuck was in trouble BIG, because the letter was smoking when he received it. It seems that his antics had bridged the ocean and he had become a celebrity back in the states, at least among the wives. He had become famous with everyone, except his wife to whom he had become infamous. What she had heard was not at all what had happened, the word having been sent back by someone who had only heard rumors, and then reported only the dark parts thereof. Chuck wrote his wife and told her the truth that he didn't remember anything of what happened. His infuriated wife wouldn't believe him when he tried to explain. It finally took letters of explanation from some of us who knew her and she trusted, to get poor Chuck off the hook.

Chuck taught us all a lesson that night. The lesson of brotherhood and respect. That when you treat someone with dignity and respect, no matter what their race or belief or station in life, it always returns in kind, sometimes coming back ten-fold.

"Would you like a flower, Madame?"

EMERGENCY PULLOUT

Unbeknown to most of the crew, the North Koreans chose the day the Hawk was to arrive at Hong Kong to shoot down an American EC-121. The North Koreans claimed the EC-121 violated their airspace, which the U.S. flatly denied. The Hawk was pulling into Hong Kong harbor when word of the incident was received. Those of us who knew were concerned about how long we would be allowed to stay. This was of particular interest for those whose wives had flown over to meet their husbands, planning to enjoy a few days in the big city. It doesn't take long for rumors to get started among the crew, and it seemed like everyone tried to get off the ship, at least for a few hours.

Anticipating some sort of punitive action by the U.S., the powers that be decided to divert some heavy firepower into the new theater of operations. The word arrived at the Hawk about 6 p.m., just after the first liberty party of about 3000 men had gone ashore. "EMERGENCY RECALL!" All hands were to report back to the ship as soon as possible. This was not as easy as it may sound. The Hawk was anchored about 30 minutes offshore. There were regular water taxies running to shuttle the troops back, but they had scattered into a city of many millions of people.

The Shore Patrol was notified and began to spread the word, return to the ship, immediately. They couldn't tell them why, other than the ship was going to get underway soon. All of the major hotels were notified to inform any personnel from the Hawk to return to the ship. Additionally, all of the personnel notified were asked to notify others they may see. Thus, the recall commenced.

I was in a large department store shopping for clothes when a fellow officer informed me of the recall. I completed my shopping and headed for the dock to catch a water taxi back to the Hawk. There was already a large group of crewmen congregating at the dock. I rarely took officer's privilege to go to the head of the line, but I hold a very responsible position and I know a lot of planning would be happening in the next few hours that would require my presence. I went to the head of the line and caught the next boat.

Back aboard the Hawk I learned we were pulling out at midnight, just three hours away. The Captain was fearful that we would leave many of the crew behind simply because they didn't get the word. As it worked out we only left 160 people who were picked up by our plane guard destroyer the next morning and brought to join us.

The USS Enterprise was pulled from Yankee station and sent direct to conduct flight operations in the waters off of North Korea. The Enterprise was a much faster ship than the Hawk, and could travel the required distance faster than we. We were the backup, and were sent to the port of Sasebo, Japan to await further orders. All precautions were to be taken so as not to provoke an international incident, but we were authorized to shoot to kill if attacked. We set up a manned alert of four F4 Phantom interceptors and an A3 tanker. We also had a number of attack aircraft loaded, ready for a launch one hour after notification. This required

AIROPS and CATCC be manned with minimum crews, in case a launch was required.

The Captain must have had some powerful orders, because he kicked the power onto all four screws. The Hawk shuttered and groaned under the stresses and we pushed speeds we didn't believe possible for a ship that size. The sea was also rougher than what we were used to. When the ship would hit a large swell, it would make a heavy rumbling sound, sometimes popping like a huge oil can. I wondered if the old girl would stay together. She did, and three days later we were in Sasebo, Japan.

DONALD L HOWE

ONE MILLION DOLLARS

As the Hawk steamed toward Japan, the plan of action for all of the forces was formulated. This plan called for the Hawk to go into port for five days at Sasebo, Japan. This was exciting for the crew, having just been pulled out of Hong Kong. One slight problem emerged. MONEY!

The U.S. forces in Japan did not use "dollars" or U.S. currency. Instead, they were issued "script", or "funny money" as it was called. This was done to curb the illegal flow of U.S. currency into Japan. When the troops were out in the local economy they used "YEN", the legal currency of Japan. There were those who would accept funny money, but they did so at great risk. Funny money was changed periodically, and when it was to change was never publicized. The locals could change funny money into yen, if the script was current. If, however, the script was out of date, the U.S. would not honor it and the local would lose out. The system worked okay. Our problem was that we were about to turn 3000 troops loose without script or yen, just dollars. This would have made both the Japanese and U.S. governments unhappy with us. Something had to be done.

It was decided that we would launch the ship's C1 one day before entering port in Sasebo, loaded with ONE MILLION DOLLARS in "green", or U.S. Currency, bound for a small Japanese Air Defense field near Sasebo. The plane would be met by the financial types from the U.S. Navy base at Sasebo who would exchange the green for funny money and Yen. The C1 would then return to the ship and TRAP before entering into the harbor. The script and Yen could then be exchanged prior to turning the troops loose, and everyone would be happy.

Now, AIROPS was a party to this plan only because we controlled the ship's C1. We were directed to find a crew and execute the operation. A financial officer from the ship would actually handle the money, all we had to do was get him there and back with the goods. Not a problem.

I think there is a part of larceny and thievery in all of us. One million dollars was a lot of money in 1970. It's a lot now. My roommate, with whom I also shared the AIROPS watch job, and I were discussing who we would get to send with this bundle of cash. We jokingly discussed the possibility of the two of us taking it, and not reaching our destination. In a surprisingly short period of time we had devised a plan of stealing the cash and splitting it three ways.

The plan was to launch, then take a course toward Okinawa. At a point near Okinawa the aircraft would suddenly develop an engine fire, which would result in having to make an emergency ditching at sea. We would not actually ditch, but would proceed into Okinawa at low altitude, ditch close to shore, and escape by blending in with the U.S. military personnel stationed there. The wreckage of the plane would not be found because it was not where we would have reported it to be. They would presume us dead after a few days and we could escape back to the States. Not much of a plan, but we were not professional crooks either. The only hitch was how we could get our wives into the picture without giving ourselves away. We would also have to get the financial type to go along with the plan as the third party.

After much discussion, we decided the plan probably wouldn't work and if we tried it we would spend the rest of our lives in Leavenworth. So, we dropped the plan. To avoid any further temptation, we assigned the flight to other pilots, but didn't tell them what their cargo would be.

I am not surprised we decided against the plan. We were descent, law-abiding men. What was surprising to me was how quickly my roommate and I were able to develop such a sinister plan, just by joking around, not realizing what we were doing until we were well down the road of treachery. I've often wondered how many others have been placed in similar circumstances of opportunity, jokingly developed a plan, then tried to carry it out, only to be caught and their lives changed forever. I don't think any man knows his limits until faced with high stakes opportunity. Most people can turn down the petty cash, but the BIG BUCKS?

We launched the C1 as planned, and the operation went off like clockwork. I don't think the assigned pilots knew they had so much cash onboard until they arrived at Sasebo, maybe not even then. Either way they returned with the funny money and Yen, and the financial officer. To my knowledge none of us has subsequently been sent to Leavenworth. But only because we are not punished for our thoughts!

JAPAN

Japan is a beautiful country. This fact was revealed as the Hawk slowly sailed into the harbor at Sasebo. The ship anchored quite far out because of the limited water depth closer in. Sasebo was not an international harbor like Hong Kong, rather it was a ship building and a fishing port. There was some commercial shipping, but on a much more limited scale. This time there wasn't any water taxis to carry the troops ashore, only the Hawk's own boats.

There was a small U.S. Naval station at Sasebo that included limited support facilities. They did have a base exchange and a nine-hole golf course, a gym, and a small dock. The action at Sasebo was in town. When I say action, I am referring to action at a level the Japanese were used to. The Japanese are a conservative, reserved people, able to get along well with each other perhaps better than any other society on earth. This probably seemed a little "flat" to many of the Hawk's sailors, but what the area lacked in party animals it made up for in scenery.

This part of Japan has terrain similar to California with weather and vegetation similar to Florida. The one difference was the ocean. The area was dotted with bays and inlets, and it was very obvious that the people gained much of their support from the sea. It was spring, just after winter's rains and summer's monsoons. It was gorgeous, especially after coming from Southeast Asia where it was HOT in the winter, and HOTTER in the summer.

The Hawk had received permission to base the ship's C1 at the same field where the money transfer had taken place. This field was about 20 miles from Sasebo, and 10 miles from the ship. Direct transportation from existing sources was not available, so we enlisted the support of the plane guard helicopter outfit. We arranged to have the HOOKIE make several transfer trips each day, to shuttle pilots and interested passengers to the C1. Sometimes two trips were required because of those wanting rides in the C1 to other places in Japan. We thus became a charter service, so to speak, flying the C1 around southern Japan. These flights were almost always visual sightseeing trips, taking in the many sights that can only be seen from the advantage of altitude.

Hiroshima, where the U.S. dropped its first atomic bomb on Japan during world war II, was only about an hour's bus ride from Sasebo. Here many of our sailors viewed the awesome destruction caused by the bomb. We as Americans were probably viewed with mixed feelings by the locals. It seemed the young people were very open, wanting to engage in conversation to practice the English they were taught in school. They were very friendly and didn't seem to carry any animosity toward us. This was not true with the older folks. They were much more reserved. They didn't throw rocks, or anything like that. They just quietly kept their distance, looking at us with suspicion. It almost seemed like they were wondering if we were the one's who had flown the plane that dropped the bomb.

Sasebo had a very extensive bus system. One could travel just about anywhere on a bus. The problem was knowing which bus to take. The bus station was centrally located, but ascertaining which bus was the one you wanted became a problem. Many busses departed from the station at the same time, and only a few signs were in English. The bus employees helped when they could, but often times they didn't speak English either. The most effective way seemed to be to tell the operators the name of the town or place you wanted to go, and they would point to the right bus. This worked most of the time, but you were never sure if you had the right bus until you reached the destination successfully. When you had to make a transfer en route, things really got complicated. I always allowed extra time to cover that lost when I would end up at the wrong place and have to come back and start over.

I always felt comfortable alone with the Japanese. It was not like the Philippines where you traveled in groups for your own safety. It was safe to walk the streets of Sasebo at night, with money in your pocket. You could trust the cashiers to give you correct change. The feeling was wholesome, like you were at home, at a safe haven. Hong Kong was not like this. Alongapo was far from this. At these places extra caution had to be exercised. Not so in Sasebo. It was safe.

Sasebo was the home of a shipbuilding industry that made "Super Tankers". These tankers, longer than the Hawk, were HUGE. We were allowed to visit the company on a non-interference basis, which proved very interesting. These "super tankers" were assembled in segments. These segments were fabricated at another location then floated over to the drydock in Sasebo where they were joined to the other segments, thus making the ship. The ships were about 1100 feet long, with a 35 to 40 feet draft when loaded. This was at a time when these super ships were brand new to the world. They could not enter many of the world's ports when loaded because the ports were too shallow. I think the most amazing thing about these ships was that they had only one screw! Speed was obviously not their concern. It was said that it would take up to 24 hours for these ships to reach their cruising speed when loaded.

I think most of us enjoyed our time at Sasebo. Many of the wives that had been left on the dock at Hong Kong were able to readjust their travel arrangements ending up in Sasebo. The pace of life was much slower throughout, and we all took advantage of the time for a good rest.

It wasn't long until we left Sasebo and relieved the Enterprise. We operated off the North Korean coast for few days, using Seoul as our BINGO field. Operations here were not the same as Yankee station. Basically, it was just to show our presence, and no bombs were carried. We did carry defensive weapons, because there was a real threat, but only on the fighters. Flight operations were good practice however, because the weather was almost always bad, and both pilots and controllers could bone UP on their instrument flying procedures. Soon the politicians and statesmen did their jobs, and determined we were not going to start another war with North Korea. The Hawk was then sent back to Sasebo.

Another week passed and things started to get boring. We had our R&R. We were ready to go back to work. The powers that be must have heard our grumbling, because they sent us back to Yankee station. We had spent almost a month away from the line, mostly acting like tourists. We were becoming soft, and we were wasting time. We were ready to put the "HAWK BACK ON THE STALK".

COLD CATS

As a carrier pilot, nothing ruins your whole day faster than a "COLD CAT SHOT". This is the term given to a catapult malfunction, where not enough PULL is given the aircraft by the catapult, resulting in too low an "END SPEED". The "END SPEED" is the airspeed the aircraft is traveling at the completion of the CAT SHOT, when it is catapulted into the air. Too LOW an END SPEED means the aircraft doesn't have enough airspeed to fly, so it simply goes off the end of the CAT and falls into the water.

COLD CAT SHOTS were a particular problem with the earlier hydraulic catapults. The Hawk had STEAM catapults, and this was rarely, if ever, a problem. The steam system utilized a tank the size of a large house as an accumulator, and a dual piston catapult. The accumulator was filled and brought up to a certain pressure. When the CAT was to be fired, the catapult Officer ensured the accumulator had the right pressure for the type (WEIGHT) of aircraft being shot, and that the pilot was ready. He then released the pressurized steam into the CAT cylinders. Once the steam was released there was no turning back. The steam drove the pistons of the CAT, accelerating the aircraft to its end speed. It made no difference to the CAT if the aircraft was or was not ready to go. When the CAT was fired, the plane went. Theoretically the aircraft could actually have no power on and its brakes set. No matter, when the CAT was shot, the plane went. Thus, the catapult Officer's job was very important. To my knowledge, the Hawk NEVER had a COLD CAT SHOT. Not true of our sister ship.

It was one of those "INKWELL" nights, with weather on the poor side to say the least. Our sister ship was operating the "CROSS" schedule from 6 p.m. to 6 a.m., so their night operations coincided with ours. This only became a problem when the two ships got too close to one another and our traffic patterns conflicted, but this was not the case this night. We were close enough to monitor their UHF radio transmissions, and had both their approach and departure control frequencies tuned in. We also monitored the "Raspberry" frequency a little closer, just in case we had to communicate. Our sister ship had HYDRAULIC catapults.

They were into their second launch, about 9:50 p.m. when they experienced a COLD CAT SHOT. The plane crashed into the water, but did not catch fire. The pilots were able to get out of the sinking craft, and were both picked up safely by their plane guard helicopter.

An unspoken brotherhood exists among all airmen and to a certain extent, the aircraft carriers are a part of this. We, of course, offered our assistance if they needed it, specifically, the assistance of our HOOKIE. They did not require our help. No one likes to see the misfortune of others, especially when it meant losing an aircraft, and MOST especially when pilots were lost. We were sad that they had this problem, but the story doesn't end here.

On the recovery following the ill-fated launch, one of the landing aircraft crashed on landing, due to the PITCHING DECK. The plane did catch fire. The pilots could not get out of the aircraft, and suffered major burns before the fire could be extinguished. This heightened our feelings for their misfortune.

Our sister ship's next launch was at 11:30 p.m. They experienced another COLD CAT SHOT. This time the pilot was not as fortunate, and could not escape the aircraft before it sank, and he was lost. This time the other ship accepted the assistance of our HOOKIE, and a search was maintained at the crash site just in case the downed pilot did get out and was missed earlier. It was unsuccessful.

I don't know if we were just lucky, had better equipment, or had a sharper crew. Whatever, we only lost six planes over a nine-month period, two of those being to hostile fire. Our sister ship lost three that night, and five others during that thirty-day line period. There ship was equipped the same as ours except for the hydraulic CATS, and the ACLS or All-Weather Carrier Landing system. It was also a little smaller overall. I know the ACLS pulled us out of hot water a few times, and we were glad we had it. We cringed each time we heard of another mishap aboard this ill-fated ship, and thanked the Lord above for our good fortune.

DONALD L HOWE

MONSOONS AND PITCHING DECKS

When the Monsoon season starts in Southeast Asia it means rain and generally poor flying conditions. Towering thunderstorms would build during the day, bring torrential rain, then taper off into a kind of in a foggy haze. The thunderstorms also brought winds that created sea swells, and led to? You guessed it, PITCHING DECKS!

It was always interesting to watch aircraft on final approach on the glide slope television, doing their little dance up and down, up and down, up and down, until finally they TRAPPED. What made it more interesting were the increased incidents of "HOOK SKIPS". A HOOK SKIP was when the aircraft landed properly but did not catch a wire. This usually occurred because the arresting hook bounced, or hit the top of an arresting cable, was somehow out of phase with the ship, or something was wrong with the hook. Whenever there was a HOOK SKIP, the arresting cables had to be visually inspected for damage before the AIR BOSS would give the "GREEN DECK" signal and recoveries resumed. If the cable was damaged it had to be removed before another aircraft could TRAP. This was necessary because a damaged wire could result in a cable failure, ruining everybody's day. If an arresting cable were to break, it could slow the aircraft below its flying speed without keeping it on the ship. The plane would simply motor over the end of the angled deck and stall, crashing into the water. The other problem with a broken arresting cable was the cable itself. When it snapped, so much energy was transmitted into the cable that it whipped around in an arc, like a giant sword, cutting everything in its path in half. If this occurs, the Arresting Officer usually pays the highest price because he is right there in front of the cable. If he is lucky, he only looses his feet.

A HOOK SKIP always results in a BOLTER for the aircraft. When an aircraft BOLTERS, very close monitoring by AIROPS follows. Most likely, the aircraft would be approaching low fuel state, needing to be "TANKED". If the aircraft were approaching low state, AIROPS would have the tanker HAWK the bird, allowing it to pull up, plug in and take fuel shortly after the BOLTER occurred. When TANKING was complete, the aircraft would rejoin the landing pattern and try again. If an aircraft had three HOOK SKIPs in a row, another aircraft was sent up to make a visual inspection of the suspect hook. If the problem was with the hook itself, the aircraft either had to be TRAPPED by the "BARRICADE" method or sent "BINGO" to a land base. We always preferred the latter when possible.

For some strange reason, HOOK SKIPs seemed to increase with PITCHING DECKS. No one could ever give me a plausible explanation of this. It just happened that way. Theoretically, it shouldn't happen at all, but it did.

It was the policy of the ship and air wing that each squadron have a qualified representative present during night and instrument recoveries. This was usually a pilot, ranging from the commanding officer to a junior officer who knew a little about their planes. The reasoning behind this was to have someone readily available in case of an emergency. This person could advise AIROPS and hopefully a suitable course of action could be implemented. When we had PITCHING

DECK conditions, these representatives were ALWAYS present, probably because unforeseen things happened then. Perhaps we all remembered the F4 that made a good approach, but ended up a pile of molten metal during our CARQUAL phase. Whatever the reason, the representatives showed up, and it was always a good opportunity for me to get to know them. Over the period of the cruise I got to know just about all the pilots from all the squadrons, and they got to know me.

I think this worked to our advantage because they also learned what information was important to the AIROPS side of the operation, and were much more willing to pass information we needed. The opportunity for these representatives to witness what went on in AIROPS and CATCC helped them to grasp the problems we faced on every instrument and night recovery. It was all too easy for a pilot to get the feeling he was flying the only plane in the sky, and he would get upset when a controller didn't seem to react soon enough on a request. After witnessing a recovery, especially one with an emergency, these pilots would oftentimes understand the magnitude of handling up to 50 planes at one time, departing and recovering. Their subsequent cooperation was notable. This was also advantageous because the pilots could see what AIROPS and CATCC could do for them, especially during an emergency.

Perhaps the most important thing gained by all who visited AIROPS was that I was not a monster, the image of which was sometimes portrayed over the intercoms. We then began having a lot more fun, which helped us all overcome the stresses of our positions. They learned that I really did care about them and their problems, and that when they called and I answered with a "you confuse me with someone who gives a s**t!", that I was only bluffing and used that answer to break the ice. I became fast friends with many of these pilots. Our verbal exchanges helped, and never interfered with the operations.

One particularly bad night, with lousy weather and a PITCHING DECK, we were attempting to recover an A6. The A6 was normally one of the easiest planes to bring aboard. Their approach was a little slower than the other planes, and the aircraft generally seemed a little more stable throughout. But, this A6 refused to be caught! After three approaches, three HOOK SKIPS and three BOLTERS, we sent the plane up to the tanker. The tanker gave the A6 2500 pounds of fuel, then dropped back to inspect the ill-fated plane's hook. All appeared to be normal. It was extending properly and everything was intact.

We brought the A6 back and entered him into the pattern. By now all the other planes had landed except the A6 and the tanker. It was the last recovery of the night, so the A6 had the entire ship to itself. Trying everything, the pilot agreed to an automatic approach. The approach was perfect, right down to the TRAP position. "HOOK SKIP, BOLTER" came across the intercom. CATCC brought the plane around again, another HOOK SKIP and BOLTER. Once again CATCC brought the bird around. It would be the bird's sixth attempt. Both the squadron rep and I agreed. If he didn't make it this time it would be a BINGO. I had the tanker HAWK the A6 as it came around this one last time. The approach was again flawless, with the aircraft touching down perfectly. Again, "HOOK SKIP, BOLTER", came over the intercom.

"Kingfisher Seven, your signal BINGO, Danang. Pull up straight ahead for tanking. Call departure control for vector when complete."

The A6 was given his instructions. The pilot didn't know why he couldn't TRAP, but after six approaches to a pitching deck he wasn't going to argue. He pulled up, took on another 2500 pounds of fuel, then went to Danang to spend the night and find out the problem. We brought the tanker aboard and called it a night.

The mechanics at the Navy detachment in Danang discovered a pinched hydraulic line to the hook actuating cylinder. The hook would extend and appear down and in position, but the hydraulic cylinder was not receiving enough fluid to keep pressure on the hook. The hydraulic system was operating properly, thus the pilot had no way of knowing there was a problem. When the hook would hit the deck on touchdown it would bounce up, and simply ride over all the wires. By the time the pilot had a chance to check his hook position indicator after waveoff, the cylinder had been able to push the hook down to its proper place and it showed down. The line was repaired, and all was well. We brought the A6 back on the first recovery the next day. It made a normal approach and TRAPPED on the first try.

DONALD L HOWE

WHO WAS THAT?

Air Traffic control around an aircraft carrier is almost always interesting, and is sometimes downright hectic. When the weather was good, the AIR BOSS controlled a visual traffic pattern where aircraft were being recovered every thirty seconds. This interval was set up by the pilots, for the most part, after much experience. If they don't leave sufficient interval between planes, they have to take a "WAVE OFF", and make another try. If they leave too much interval, it delays the recovery and creates a dangerous situation where the second plane in line doesn't see the first, and cuts him off coming around on final. The AIR BOSS watches very carefully for this, usually sending the guilty party around for another approach.

When the weather was not so good, or at night, all the recoveries are made using the instrument recovery method. Now, the Carrier Air Traffic Control Center, or CATCC is responsible for maintaining the separation between aircraft, and bringing them down for landings.

Carrier Air Controllers are blessed, or cursed, with a certain pride that comes with mastery of a very difficult coordination problem. When they have done their job correctly everything works like clockwork. All the planes should be spaced properly, with one arriving on the "BALL" every minute. This is primarily the Approach controller's job. He is responsible for bringing the planes down from altitude and must know where every plane is located within his airspace. No one is allowed to cross thru this airspace unless they are under his control. The approach controller brings the aircraft into about three miles and transfers control to one of two final controllers. Occasionally, any one of these controllers screws up. The biggest problem is they lose track of, or misidentify an airplane. When this happens things really become confused. There is, of course, a supervisor that is older and wiser, that never gets confused, or so they say. His job is to pull it all back together when the individual controller screws up.

One dark, cloudy night a recovery was in progress. Everything was proceeding normally, all under control. Several aircraft had TRAPPED, and the remaining were in line, stretched out about 20 miles, proceeding inbound.

"I have an unidentified contact at six miles, paralleling our course, altitude unknown!"

The approach controller who barked this information could just as well have dropped a live hand grenade in the room. All of CATCC went into an uproar. Where did this guy come from? Who was he? Would he remain clear of our recovery pattern? What was his altitude? Did anyone have contact with the bogey? Was this the tanker? Did anyone have a lost COM (radio failure)? Where is he going? Final control, do you have him? The supervisor was going six different directions at the same time. The approach controller had the presence of mind not to focus his attention on the "unident" (unidentified aircraft) and kept his other birds in line.

A final controller bringing in another aircraft bellowed, "I have the bogey on my radar. He is clear of landing aircraft."

Our search radar was great until a target got within three miles of the ship. At this point is just disappears off the screen. The ship's surface search radar worked a lot better close in but we didn't have it set up on a repeater. The final controller's radar had a very narrow window, and he only saw targets that flew into it.

The unidentified target then flew by the ship.

The AIR BOSS called. "What was that?"

I didn't have any answers.

The unidentified aircraft then disappeared off all our radar scopes as fast as it appeared. I called CIC. They had not picked up the target. I checked with the departure controller. He did not have the target. No one had the target. It was gone, or was it? I notified the Captain and he called "General Quarters". We tried every piece of radar on the ship. We even had an airborne E2 aircraft try to find the phantom. No one could pick up the target.

I called the AIR BOSS back and asked what he had seen. He described the aircraft as a large, multi-engine jet aircraft. It flew past the ship at about 300 feet altitude, paralleling our course. We didn't have anything like that in the naval arsenal. Could it have been a B52? It certainly wasn't an airliner. They never flew at that low an altitude, except to land, and they all knew there was a war going on. Could it have been a navy P3 patrol plane? Could it have been a Russian, or Chinese? It was considered at one point running an intercept with an F4. This turned out to be redundant because we couldn't find the unident anyway.

A full report of the incident was made. A search of all the local commands was made to ascertain if one of their planes had been in the area. The pass was made just like the photography runs I used to make in patrol planes, but the nearest P3 had been 400 miles away. It was NOT one of ours, or at least no one would admit it.

The big question was not who he was, or why he didn't call us while in our airspace. The big question was why we didn't see the unident on our radar. We saw everything else.

We didn't even have any fuzzy contacts. Our gear was operating perfectly, but we didn't see that plane!

It took some effort but we were able to calm the CATCC supervisor. Nothing like this had ever happened to him before. Nothing like this had ever happened to any of us before. An unidentified aircraft passing through your final recovery pattern, unannounced, was tantamount to total disaster for an air controller. It was worse for the supervisor. Neither would be able to live down the shame of the day. Both would be twice as cautious next time.

The incident did have one positive side effect. It brought us back to reality. We realized that even though we felt invincible, we were quite vulnerable. That unidentified aircraft could just as easily have turned a little to the left and dropped a string of bombs across our flight deck. We could have been had without even firing a shot! Had this happened, the survivors, not the AIR BOSS, would have been the ones asking the question from their watery perch, "WHO WAS THAT?"

MAN OVERBOARD

When sailors are away from home for extended periods of time, situations develop that sometimes cause severe depression. Everyone has their ups and downs, but fortunately only a few really get into the depression category. For most of us we were so busy that we had little time to think about being away from home, but this wasn't true for all.

Officers and Petty Officers are trained to notice those sailors that are having a particularly hard time. Steps are then taken to help the depressed individual, ranging from simple counseling to professional help. Most of the time a little extra effort on the part of one's shipmates was all it took to help an individual feel wanted and a part of the group. Occasionally, an individual would turn up that others just couldn't seem to help.

Another problem affecting the morale of a sailor was the "Dear John" letter received from a girlfriend, or occasionally a spouse. No one can help with these other than just being a friend and offering a shoulder to cry on. About one in twenty fell victim to the "Dear John", usually within the first three months of a cruise. The sailor who could realize that he really didn't have anything going with the "Dear John" sender, and could start anew, was the lucky one. Those who could not accept this had serious problems. On rare occasions a sailor would be given leave to work out these problems. Usually leave was only given for a death or serious illness in the immediate family.

The ship had been deployed about seven months when one night the "Man Overboard" signal was heard over the public address system. It seems someone observed another jump off the fantail of the ship. The captain ordered an immediate search to be conducted by the plane guard destroyer following the Hawk. We were not conducting flight operations at the time, so getting a helicopter into the air took a few extra minutes.

The procedure for "Man Overboard" beyond starting a search with available resources, was to take a muster of all hands to determine who was missing. With 5500 men and thousands of nooks and crannies on the ship, this was no easy feat. Since it was during our normal sleep time, not everyone heard the "Man Overboard" signal and did not respond to the muster. A responsible Officer or petty Officer then had to go and find each missing person. A telephone call was not sufficient -- it had to be a sight muster. This muster is to be accomplished in the minimum amount of time possible to avoid unnecessary searching effort. It had happened in the past that someone reported a "Man Overboard", after observing another throw a bag of trash over the side in the dark.

When the muster was complete, it was found that indeed, we were one person short. The search was intensified, with another destroyer from a sister carrier and our own HOOKIE joining in. The two ships and the helicopter searched for the next three hours without success. It was concluded that since the sailor jumped off the fantail he would have landed in the ship's wake. The wake of a carrier immediately behind the ship is extremely turbulent, and the probability of the missing person having been immediately carried down under the water was very great. Our plane guard destroyer continued the search for an additional twelve hours. The other destroyer was sent back to its own ship and our HOOKIE returned to cover our flight operations.

An investigation was launched to determine the whys and wherefores of this individual's apparent suicide. It seems he was one of the few that slipped by his superiors and shipmates. He didn't leave a "suicide" note, but a "Dear John" letter was found in his personal effects. None of his shipmates knew of this -- they only noticed he had been a little extra quiet for a few days before he jumped overboard. He had been doing his job well, and other than this added solemnity, appeared normal.

A situation like this affects everyone on the ship, even if they didn't know the missing sailor personally. Everyone becomes more aware of those around them. Everyone seems to go the extra mile in reaching out to others. One also watches a little more closely after "Mail Call", to see if a shipmate seems distressed. We all seemed to become more caring. We also felt a feeling of having failed, failed to meet the needs of a brother who just couldn't face it any more. We all had similar problems, but some just felt isolated. We had not seen this person's problem, and we had lost him.

How important is the trust between a man and a woman? Military people face this question every time they depart on a deployment or other separation from their loved ones. It is sometimes impossible for young people to face, and know that life will go on even if this trust is broken. In our attempts to be strong we sometimes forget that "no man is an island." When this happens and we isolate ourselves, we tread on shaky ground. In this state we may not have the strength or resource to carry on in the face of adversity.

I would like to think the death of this sailor on the Hawk was not in vain. True, he couldn't face life as it presented itself at that particular moment. But, he had served his country well for at least the year he had been assigned to the Hawk. He had the courage to defend his country during a time when many protested, even went to other countries to avoid having to serve. He didn't ask for his lot in life anymore than any of US do, but he had the courage to respond to his country's needs when it called, and didn't run away. Thankfully, it is not our lot to judge the actions of this sailor. We need only remember, he was a HERO in his own right.

GOOD MORNING, ADMIRAL!

Very Important Persons, or VIPS, are a continuous happening aboard a carrier. The Hawk was no exception. We had done our job very well, and the war was winding down, a perfect chance for VIPS to visit. VIPS ran the gambit of popular political life -- reporters, correspondents, USO personnel, congressmen, senators, foreign dignitaries, allies, and our own military brass, among others. It seemed like we had some kind of VIP coming aboard everyday on the mail COD plane. It was one of my jobs as AIROPS to coordinate these visits and make sure they were handled properly thru the Air Transfer Officer who worked for us.

It happened one day that the VIP coming aboard was CINCPAC. In English, the Commander-In-Chief Pacific, or the big, big boss over the entire pacific, including the Vietnam War. Now when someone of this horsepower comes aboard everything is planned to the second, and heaven help those who screw up!

The plan was to conduct a normal launch, bring the C2 COD plane with the Admiral aboard in for a TRAP first, have him deplane and be met by our own Admiral and his staff, our captain and the ship's senior officers. The entire

145

party was then to proceed to the Admiral's offices to greet the arriving CINCPAC properly, out of the noise of the flight deck. Once the entire party was clear of the flight deck we could then start our normal recovery. Because of the rank and position of this visitor, many senior officers were in on the planning of this event.

When the time came for the launch and recovery everything was in position. The Admiral's plane arrived and was holding, ready to join the pattern and recover first. The launch began and proceeded as planned. At the proper moment, the AIRBOSS directed the Admiral's plane to initiate its recovery procedures. The plane then began a turn so as to set it up on final approach to the ship.

About this same time, we shot an A7 off the bow CAT. No sooner had the plane launched when he reported a complete failure of his primary hydraulic system. This is very significant because the flight controls of the A7 were hydraulically actuated. The plane had a backup system that would give it SEVEN minutes of flight time. We had to get him aboard within that seven minutes.

During normal visual operations both the AIRBOSS and AIROPS monitor the departure frequency. The AIRBOSS called before I had a chance to call him, asking what I wanted to do? I told him to wave off the Admiral and take the A7, then bring the Admiral back as soon as possible. BOSS then asked if I wanted to tell the staff or did I want him to do it? I told him I would make the call. I never got the chance.

The Admiral's plane broke off their approach on short final, adding power and turning to the right to go around. The greeting party stood on the flight deck and watched the plane go around, probably sure their naval careers were going to come to a quick end. I had just been informed of another emergency and became involved with it. Soon my "Hot Line" telephone rang with the Chief of Staff, a Navy captain, on the other end. He asked what the hell I was doing and I told him I had an emergency and couldn't talk to him, then hung up the phone.

The crippled A7 turned onto short final, picked up the BALL and made a normal recovery. Two F4'S were behind the A7, then the Admiral's plane. All TRAPPED aboard and the Admiral was met by the ship's greeting party, but this time it was over the noise of the flight deck with aircraft operating. The brass was not very happy. When I got the chance, I called the captain and explained what had happened. He was not upset, and thanked me for doing what had to be.

A few minutes later my counterpart from the staff appeared before me and demanded that I go with him to see the Chief of Staff. Another emergency had developed during this time and I could not leave. I informed him of the same and replied I would come up as soon as the recovery was complete, as there was no one to relieve me at my post. He stormed off. I remained at AIROPS until I felt I could leave my post in the hands of an officer-in-training, then went up to see the Chief of Staff.

The Chief of Staff sat at his desk. There were two other Navy captains, a commander, my boss and my staff counterpart present in the room. I reported my presence in the most proper military manner I knew. The chief of Staff then stood up and began to chew me out. He chewed for five minutes, never asking for an explanation, getting more excited as he talked. He then asked if I had anything to say.

Now basically I am a pretty cool person, to handle AIROPS you had to be. But I do get upset when I am faced with absurdity in the name of protocol, which doesn't mean anything anyway. I answered: "Yes sir. I just ordered a maneuver that saved a two-million-dollar aircraft and maybe a man's life. I was correct in what I ordered, and if it happens again tomorrow, I will do it again the same way!" With that I turned and left the office, going back to my post.

When I got back to my station I thought of what I said and how I said it. I was due to leave the ship soon anyway, but wondered now if I would be leaving sooner, under guard. I didn't have long to worry about it because another emergency developed and I became lost in the job. The weather had turned bad and our operations had to upgrade to instrument control.

That evening during a recovery, I was again involved with an emergency that took all my attention. I heard someone call "Attention on deck", but paid no attention. When I could look up I saw more Admiral's stars than I dreamed possible. I stood UP at attention and greeted the Admiral.

"Are you the guy who sent me around?"

What could I say? "Yes sir!"

"YOU know, you were right!" He said.

"Yes sir, I know." Finally, someone who thinks more about getting the job done right, rather than being dominated by fear and protocol. I went on to talk to the Admiral for about 10 minutes, explaining what happened and the possible consequences to the A7. We also talked about other things and about AIROPS in general. He was an alright fellow and I enjoyed the conversation. Another emergency checked in and the Admiral excused himself.

I expected to hear more of the incident but never did -- not from my captain nor from the staff. I had made a promise to myself many months earlier that I would do my best to get the job done, but not at the expense of men's lives or equipment, if possible. This sometimes put VIPS in a secondary category. I knew that any good commander would realize that the operation ALWAYS came first and individuals second, regardless of their position. In my mind, the convenience of all the VIPS combined were not worth the life of one man. I followed that policy, and could always sleep well at night.

AN OCEAN OF DOLPHINS

Nature has a way of playing tricks on man. Not the kind of tricks that affect us directly, but the kind that hit us just when we think we have seen it all, reducing our puny reality back into its proper perspective.

We had dolphins as companions for the entire cruise. Usually six to twelve at a time, frolicking back and forth across the bow wave. It almost seemed like a challenge to a speed race. The dolphins would come along side of the ship, swimming with their "big brother", then with a burst of speed pull ahead switching from one side of the bow to the other. They would then drop back and kind of look at the ship as though they were wondering why it hadn't accepted the challenge and joined the race. Occasionally, they would all fan out, heading away from the ship in a sunburst fashion until they would all disappear. Then a few moments later they would all return, lining up in formation along the bow wave. One could observe these magnificent creatures just about anytime there was enough light to see. This did not prepare us however, for what we were to see as we approached the California coast.

It was time to launch the air wing. All of the aircraft that were flyable were to launch and proceed to their respective air stations. There was little wind, so the launch was made on the heading toward home. We were close enough to shore that it was just a short hop to their bases. All but two planes could be launched. It seemed strange to launch almost 100 planes and not recover a single one. The launch went without a hitch.

With the aircraft gone, we were getting antsy, wanting to get home, and the ship just didn't seem to go fast enough. Many of us were up on deck, pacing, like waiting for a child to be born. Anything to make the time pass. Frequently we would look ahead for a sign of land, only to see the expanse of ocean along the horizon.

Something seemed strange. The ocean ahead seemed to froth, not just in spots like that caused by the wind, but the entire ocean. We were heading directly into it. For that matter, the frothing stretched as far as the eye could see in both directions. As we got closer a wonder of nature could be discerned. It was dolphins! Not just a few, but thousands upon thousands of dolphins!

Soon we were in the midst of what had appeared to be a huge school of dolphins. We discovered they were not alone. They were chasing tuna! For every dolphin that jumped there were a dozen tuna. From a distance all we could see was the dolphins, but the frothing was actually caused by the tuna. I don't know if the dolphins were actually chasing the tuna or they were just swimming together. It didn't matter. What was important was the sheer numbers of fish and dolphins in the school. They stretched left, right and ahead to the horizons.

We steamed through this massive school for twenty full minutes, seemingly cutting it in half. With the ship steaming at twenty-one knots this made the school at least seven miles wide! Estimating we could see at least ten miles in each direction, the school had to be over twenty miles long! Never in my wildest imagination would I have guessed there were that many fish in the entire Pacific Ocean, let alone in one school!

Perhaps had we seen these creatures at some other time it would have been even more impressive. As magnificent as it was, it was not the most important thing on our minds. Just after clearing this huge school of fish we spotted land. It was the pacific coast, the hills of Southern California. We were coming home.

HOME PORT

It was a bright clear day. The hills of Point Loma seemed to stand out as a giant guidepost. San Diego and the surrounding cities gleamed seemingly as they had never done before. It was glorious!

The Hawk approached the entrance to the harbor slowly, but with determination. A thousand sailors in full dress uniform lined her flight deck. Passing boats honked their horns, their passengers waving and saluting. Cars lined the streets next to the water's edge with people cheering. Ships anchored in the harbor gave their salutes. A mighty warrior was returning home.

As the Hawk made the last turn before reaching its dock the waiting loved ones could be seen. Thousands and thousands of wives, children, parents and friends waited to greet their own with a hero's welcome. There was a band playing with a reception

As sailors were released from their duty to line the flight deck, they came rushing to the side next to the dock. Hundreds more came from the inside of the ship to wave and greet their loved ones. It seemed like it took hours to complete the docking procedure and get the gangplanks in place. Reunions still seemed an eternity away.

For nine months the Hawk had guarded the seas. For nine months her crew and their loved ones had waited for this moment. Babies had been born in their absence. Children had grown older and taller. Each family had their own story to tell. A lot of catching up was to be done. For some, coming home was not to be a pleasant thing. For all there was the reestablishment of relationships put on hold nine months earlier. Would things still be the same? Did absence make the heart grow fonder? Did absence make the heart grow fonder, for somebody else? Would young children remember their fathers? Each had their questions. Each had their excitement. But for all, the time of waiting was over.

With gangplanks in place, it was announced that all hands not on duty could go ashore. Like a burgeoning stream, the sailors began pouring from the ship. They were met by loving sweethearts who jumped into their arms, children who attacked their fathers in a swarm, and parents who thankfully reclaimed a son from the hands of war. Many tears were shed, mostly tears of happiness and joy. The Hawk was home!

Vietnam was not a popular war. It was not uncommon for those in uniform to be spat upon or hit by eggs and tomatoes as they walked in public places. Friends turned upon friends when they joined or were drafted into the military. Many looked upon those in uniform as warmongers and insensitive killers. Many considered them to be the cause of the war, not understanding how little the individual soldier or sailor had a say in the matter. Those against the U.S. being in Vietnam seemed to forget that wars were the result of failed diplomacy and politics, not by actions of the military. Those against the war never seemed to realize how demoralizing their actions were upon individual soldiers and sailors, especially if they had at one time been good friends.

But, none of this was here today. Today the Hawk and its sailors were heroes. They had fought the good fight and earned their rest. They had met the rigors of war with honor. They could meet their loved ones with love and dignity. They could return home distinguished, having done their duty as well or better than anyone. Many had left as boys, but returned as men. Today they could proudly hold their heads high. Today they could say with pride and honor, "THE HAWK IS MY SHIP!"

ABOUT THE AUTHOR

Donald L. Howe joined the navy in 1958, attended flight school through the Naval Aviation Cadet Program, receiving his commission and wings in 1960. As a junior officer he was assigned to patrol Squadron TWO, based at NAS Whidbey Island, Washington. As a pilot, then LTJG (Lieutenant Junior Grade) Howe became a Plane Commander and was assigned his own crew for the final 18 months in the squadron. He then attended the US Naval postgraduate school in Monterey, California, and was awarded a bachelor of Science degree. His next assignment was as an accident investigator. In this position 15 major accident reports were compiled and published, but perhaps more important for Mr. Howe, he discovered his ability and desire to write.

As Lieutenant Commander Howe, two-and-one-half years were spent aboard the USS Kitty Hawk, CVA 63, as Assistant Air Operations Officer. During this assignment his primary duty was Air Operations watch officer. The Air Operations watch officer is the individual responsible for coordination of the entire air operation within 50 miles of an aircraft carrier, including supervision over the carrier Air Traffic Control Center. All air operations were, in one form or another, coordinated by AIROPS. Thus, he became the "insider" qualified to write this work.

Since his naval career Mr. Howe has been involved with civilian industry in the construction field as a production Coordinator. His position again put him into the "Heart" of operations. His desire to write was always present being used to writing newsletters, business proposals, specifications and contracts, etc. The pressures of his career and raising eight children didn't allow time to write about the Hawk.

After fourteen successful years in the construction field, alas, the recession of the 90's hit. Mr. Howe was subsequently afforded the time to write about his experiences, and "THE HAWK IS MY SHIP" was born.

Made in the USA
Las Vegas, NV
07 July 2021

26094644R00095